Awaken The Lion

Awaken The Lion

Reclaiming What is
Naturally Yours

LENORE PEARSON

AWAKEN THE LION
Copyright © 2024 by Lenore Pearson

All rights reserved. Printed in Australia. No part of this book may be used or reproduced in any manner whatsoever without the written permission of the author except for the use of brief quotations embodied in critical articles and book reviews.

First Edition, 2024

ISBN 978-0-6484931-1-2

Indie Published by Lenore Pearson

Cover Design: Damian Cessario

CONTENTS

Author Note ix
Introduction xi

Part 1—Self-Awareness

Chapter 1	*Leo*	3
Chapter 2	*The Mane Thing*	7
Chapter 3	*Lion Tamers*	11
Chapter 4	*When Lions Get Crabs*	15
Chapter 5	*Raising Cubs*	19
Chapter 6	*Purr-fectionism is a Lie*	25
Chapter 7	*Stop Lion to Yourself*	29
Chapter 8	*Scaredy Cat*	33
Chapter 9	*Ferocity*	37
Chapter 10	*Licking Your Wounds*	41
Chapter 11	*Lion-Hearted*	45

Part 2—Self-Acceptance

Chapter 12	*The Hunt*	51
Chapter 13	*Lion and Lioness*	55
Chapter 14	*Your Pride*	61
Chapter 15	*Marking Your Territory*	65
Chapter 16	*Be Comfortable in Your Own Fur*	71
Chapter 17	*Purr-poseful Intentions*	75
Chapter 18	*The Lion Sleeps Tonight*	81
Chapter 19	*Roarsome*	85
Chapter 20	*Curiosity Did Not Kill the Cat*	89
Chapter 21	*Pawsative Energy*	93
Chapter 22	*Prepare for the Uproar*	97

Part 3—Self-Expression

Chapter 23	*It's a Jungle Out There*	103
Chapter 24	*Hear Me Roar*	107
Chapter 25	*Your Highest Purr-tential*	111
Chapter 26	*One in a Mil-lion*	115
Chapter 27	*The Lion's Den*	117
Chapter 28	*Dande-lion*	121
Chapter 29	*Leaving Your Paw Print*	125
Chapter 30	*The Cowardly Lion*	127
Chapter 31	*Radical Rebel-lion*	129
Chapter 32	*Paws for Reflection*	133
Chapter 33	*Reclaiming the Throne*	135
The Tail End		139

Acknowledgements	143
About the Author	145

*For Dallas who has unwavering faith in me
and my work and who is living proof that
you don't have to meet someone in
person to be forever connected.*

*And for my dear friend Mitch,
who had the heart of a lion.*

AUTHOR NOTE

The words contained within this book are my personal thoughts and truths, and I stand unapologetically behind them. However, in recognition of the diverse readership this book may attract, I acknowledge that not every idea and experience presented will necessarily strike a chord with everyone. I have the utmost respect for the diversity of experience in this world. Take from this book what you will and apply it for the betterment of your own personal transformation, for this is the spirit in which it was written.

INTRODUCTION

As I sat down to write the introduction to this book, I couldn't help but be amused by the realisation that multiple personalities played a role in its creation. Though it bears a single author's name, this book is truly the product of three vastly different people, each one shaped by the twists and turns of life over the years. Reflecting on this journey, it became clear that what began as one person's story became a collaboration of distinct voices, all sharing the same name.

The version of myself that finished this book stands in stark contrast to the one who began it, a version heavily shaped by a decade filled with grief, anger, resentment, and an intense need to prove myself to others. A decade that rolled me into a ball, kicked me around, sent me flying through the air with no soft landing, broke me in half and fed me to the lions. There was an overwhelming amount of self-loathing, loyalties were tested, loss was a prominent theme, and I constantly doubted my ability to change anything in my life or become the person I desperately wanted to be. To put it bluntly, it was an absolute shit-show.

But it was also a time of awakening.

To "awaken" can mean different things to different people - waking up, beginning to notice something or becoming conscious and aware. For me, however, it meant finally getting exhausted and fed up with the ten-tonne bag of crap I had been carrying around.

One of my all-time favourite writers, Elizabeth Gilbert, once said "I've never seen any life transformation that didn't begin with the person in question finally getting tired of their own bullshit". Up until the day of my 'bullshit reckoning', I was driven by fear. My body operated in a constant state of hyper-vigilance, trying to control everything around me because the thought of anything else going wrong in my life was unbearable. Fear consumed me - I went to bed with it, woke up with it, parented with it, and I came to believe that my way of loving others was rooted in fear. Then I had a dream. It was one of those frustrating dreams that jolts you awake yet leaves the details just out of reach. But one thing lingered, echoing in my mind: "Growth and change will set you free".

This simple yet profound truth highlighted that growth requires change, and to bring about that change, I needed a level of self-awareness that would force me to confront aspects of myself I wasn't sure I would like. In the chapters that follow, you'll see how my personal transformation was shaped by new experiences, shifting perspectives and, at times, moments of great discomfort, all of which have altered my view of the world and my place in it. Writing this book has become a reflection of my evolving identities, offering a layered exploration of how time and change reveal the essence of who you really are.

Throughout this book, you'll find honest truths I've come to accept about myself and how I've shifted my perspective on life, other people and most importantly, myself. These changes have created a powerful alchemy of transformation, turning my "bullshit" into gold. As you embark on your own journey toward becoming your true self, I offer three essential pillars to help you navigate deep transformation:

- **Self-Awareness** - knowing yourself.
- **Self-Acceptance** - owning yourself.
- **Self-Expression** - being yourself.

One of the most liberating lessons I've learned from working through these areas is the importance of embracing one's shadows and imperfections. Standing strong in who you are and knowing yourself deeply can be incredibly freeing. When you fully accept and understand your own flaws and strengths, you become impervious to others' attempts to use your vulnerabilities against you. Embracing your true self, imperfections and all, allows you to navigate life's challenges with confidence and authenticity.

As a coach, I often observe a deep-seated need in people to be heard, yet many struggle with self-expression. Someone who doesn't feel heard, fails to embrace their truth, or fears showing their inner strength is like a lion without its roar. A lion's roar represents power, confidence, and the assertion of presence. Similarly, when a person expresses themselves or finds their voice, they assert their identity, communicate their true feelings, and claim their space in the world. Just as a roar announces the lion's presence, authentic self-expression enables individuals to confidently navigate their lives, establish their place, and engage with the world on their terms. What it really comes down to is tapping into your own inner lion.

There is no shame in desiring more from your life. Eventually, the weight of holding onto the facade of who you pretend to be becomes far heavier than standing strong in the truth of who you really are. Can you feel it? There is a fierce leonine energy that dwells in the soul of each and every human. This book is a call to courage - a call to step into your greatness.

The moment to harness that energy is now.

PART ONE

Self-Awareness

Know Yourself

Who are you? Who do you want to be?

Dr Phil McGraw said, "You can't change what you don't acknowledge".

This first part is a deep dive into the inner workings of you. It's about getting comfortable with all your quirks and nuances. It's discovering an appreciation for what impacts you deeply. Change cannot happen unless you first have awareness of the areas of your life that need changing. It's only then that you can make plans for what to do about it. At the end of each of the chapters to follow, there is a self-awareness question to reflect on and begin your deep dive.

CHAPTER ONE

LEO

I am a Leo.

The spirited fire sign!
A Leo personality can be defined by some of these traits:

Protective
Willing to fight
A brave and fierce leader
Poised
Theatrical
Fiery
Passionate
Loyal
Strong
Fierce
Determined
Courageous

Your star sign is one of your defining details like your name, date of birth, and address. It's something almost all people know about themselves. Often, it seems to be one of those leading conversation starters when you are getting to know someone more intimately. We bond over star signs, we make judgements based on them, we blame the unfolding events of life on them. We tend to own the strong, positive or light traits that our sign suggests and gloss over the negative, weaker or shadow traits. We often forget that, in our human complexity, we could be any one of a hundred different traits regardless of what our signs tell us. For me, as a Leo, I can be as much a Virgo or Aquarius depending on my energy, mood or situation.

I get a kick out of exploring the traits of star signs, but I don't believe our lives should be dictated by them. The truth is that, regardless of what star sign you are, every unique quality listed for each exists in everyone to some degree. There are some Leo traits that I wholeheartedly embrace and there are some that I cringe at because I don't readily identify with them. However, we all have this beautiful duality of light and shade within us. The cringe-worthy traits are the ones that live in the shadow of the psyche. We don't want to acknowledge or consciously express them because we feel they are, in some ways, shameful. But they are still there and are still able to influence us.

There is a pivotal scene from Disney's *The Lion King* that illustrates this well. Mufasa imparts a profound lesson to young Simba, showing him the vast kingdom that stretches across everything the light touches. He explains that this land is his to protect, but also warns of the shadowy place beyond their borders - a realm Simba must never venture into. I believe this moment goes beyond the surface of a simple tale of good versus evil; it is a metaphor for the light and shadow within every person. Mufasa's words emphasise the delicate balance that exists not only in the natural world but within ourselves. As a king, or simply as an individual, one must understand and respect this balance, acknowledging both the light and shadow within to truly embrace one's place in the world.

This can be hugely uncomfortable, as shining a light on your shadowy side can cause you to feel great shame for what you find there. However, to be truly authentic, you need to allow all aspects of yourself to coexist and find a healthy respect for them. You will never know when one of your shadowy traits will be one of your greatest assets. Owning your shadows is about embracing your duality and when you embrace that duality you free yourself from the behaviours and beliefs that can potentially bring you down.

In her book *The Dark Side of the Light Chasers*, Debbie Ford says that embracing your shadows involves learning how to give all of who you are permission to exist. It's not about getting rid of things you dislike about yourself but finding the positive side of these aspects.

Have you ever looked into the eyes of a lion? There's a profound sense of knowing in them. Though a lion isn't the tallest, largest, or smartest animal, his attitude and presence are undeniable. It's this commanding aura that earns him the title of King of the Jungle. We can become the kings (or queens) of our own jungles. What it takes is truly knowing who we are but, importantly, who we are not!

Having explored my Leo tendencies I have learnt that the lighter side of my personality can be creative, confident, loyal, affectionate, romantic and fun but the shadowy side can be vain, arrogant, hedonistic, dictatorial, extravagant and snobbish. I was in two minds as to whether or not to admit to those but then I wouldn't be a very good example for what I am trying to communicate here, now would I?

But what if we turn those undesirables into character strengths:

- Vain - pride in how one looks could also be understood as not being influenced by how other people look.
- Arrogant - exaggerated sense of one's self-importance could also be understood as knowing your worth.
- Hedonistic - devoted to the pursuit of pleasure could also be understood as enjoying the good things in life.
- Dictatorial - a ruler with total power could also be understood as displaying leadership qualities.
- Extravagant - lacking restraint in spending money or using resources could also be understood as not being restrained by money.
- Snobbish - having an attitude of thinking you are better than other people could be understood as being introverted and taking care with who you give your energy to.

The only way you will grow is to meet yourself in the discomfort and the discomfort is where you begin to own your shadows so you can confidently and proudly step into the light.

SELF AWARENESS CHECK-IN

What traits are you hiding in the shadows? How can you look at these differently?

CHAPTER TWO

The Mane Thing

The more you push me, the more I dig my heels in.

If you're going to understand me on a deeper level, there is an important fact you should know: I have a strong aversion to being told what to do. This isn't just about disliking direct orders; it extends to how I feel about others imposing their expectations on me, especially when those expectations exceed the standards I set for myself. I value my autonomy and the boundaries I've established, and I find it frustrating when people expect me to conform to their ideas or demands that don't align with my own goals and limits.

Some may see this as defiance, but I prefer to think of it as maintaining integrity of who I am and the life I choose to live. It is allowing space to get comfortable with being uncomfortable. I like to do things on my own terms. After carefully weighing up my options, drafting pros and cons lists, creating mind maps and detailed diagrams, and consulting with both my higher self and sometimes my husband, I make my decision. The key takeaway here is that the decision is mine to make.

Just like the decision is yours to make. You have a choice. You can either continue down the same path, experiencing the same results day after day, or you can choose to be courageous, confront your challenges, push through the discomfort and face your "bullshit", to find the gold.

I was faced with this exact situation shortly after my daughter was born, during one of the darkest periods of my life. I felt utterly alone in my journey through motherhood and blamed everyone and everything for how miserable I was. Then, one morning, I made a decision - I refused to keep feeling that way. I could have waited for the feeling to pass, but I knew I had to change things immediately. Once I made that decision, I took action. The action led to intense discomfort, but after the discomfort came the transformation.

From an early age, I realised that my own expectations have far more impact on my life than those of others. I only get truly upset with myself when I fail to meet my own standards, not when I fall short of others' expectations. Though my expectations can sometimes be impossibly high, I'm grateful to come from a line of strong-willed women who taught me to stay true to myself, regardless of what others expect.

The 'mane' thing you need to know is that transformation begins with a decision. The chapters that follow aren't intended to provide a blueprint for change, but rather to offer a new perspective to ignite your transformation. Life doesn't owe you anything; instead, you owe it to your life to live up to your fullest potential. Embracing this mindset is the first step towards meaningful change.

The most important work you will ever do is the work you do on yourself. Within you right now is the power to not only better yourself but contribute to the global shift of bettering humanity.

All you have to do is decide.

SELF AWARENESS CHECK-IN

Where in your life are you not calling the shots? Decide to change that.

CHAPTER THREE

Lion Tamers

The more people try to tame me, the louder I roar.

At the time of writing this chapter, there was breaking news from Sydney's Taronga Zoo that five lions had escaped from their enclosure. The report stated that everyone on site was moved to safety and that the lions were escorted back to their enclosure where they were being closely monitored.

They were clearly after a 'roaring good time' (Ha).

As a writer, I naturally view everything as potential content. So, I saw this as an opportunity to delve into the idea of taming one's wild spirit. On closer observation, this event reflected to me how society tries to tame those who resist conformity. These lions were simply embracing their natural instincts: the desire to roam freely. Have you ever felt the natural instinct to break free from the confines of your cage, only to be ushered back into conformity?

I frequently observe this scenario among my students and clients. Many times, they stand at the edge of a precipice, poised to take off, only to be hindered by the limitations imposed by others. It often requires some time for them to realise that the real barrier is not the limitations others place on them, but the limitations they place on themselves as a result.

No one can truly tame you without your consent. It's convenient to blame others for taming you, as it allows you to sidestep responsibility for making, what can sometimes be, some really scary changes. Comfort and complacency make blaming others an easy excuse, but it also keeps you stuck in the 'safe' zone.

Much like the lions that were guided back to their enclosure and closely monitored for everyone's safety, I've encountered situations where I too felt nudged back into a metaphorical cage. What initially seemed like others attempting to lessen my sense of self and keep me playing small was, in reality, my own willingness to remain within the safety of that cage and shield myself from disapproval.

I soon discovered that my natural free-spirited soul longed for freedom, much like the lions at Taronga Zoo. I have a strong aversion to being restricted and constrained in what I say and do. Sooner or later, that intrinsic wildness will surface, regardless of my own or anyone else's approval.

Taming, at its core, is about control, whether it originates from self-imposed limitations or external influences. Awareness of who is responsible for the taming is vital, as more often than not, you are the one enforcing the limitations and keeping yourself caged in. Unlike the lions at the zoo, you have the power to break free.

When others impose limitations, seek to understand why. What motivates people to exercise control over everything and everyone? Why does your boss demand tasks be done a certain way? Why is your spouse discontent with your choice of friends? Why does your family insist on upholding traditions without room for change? By exploring these questions, you gain fresh perspectives, enabling you to better evaluate them against your own values, desires and needs. This, in turn, empowers you to make thoughtful and informed decisions that align more closely with your authentic self (more on this in Part 2).

As you become more aware, you may realise there could be valid reasons behind your boss's preferences for working in a particular way. It's possible that your spouse's concerns about your friends stem from their perception that these friendships don't enrich your life. In the same vein, your family traditions may, upon reflection, reveal themselves as a beautiful means of nurturing closeness and belonging. With this insight, you then get to decide on your own terms, whether this 'taming' is aligned with what you want.

Conversely, self-imposed constraints can present significant barriers to your personal growth. In my experience, these limitations often originate from your own beliefs and fears. Once you have gained awareness of these factors, you can actively challenge them and break free of them.

Shortly after my first book's release, a well-intentioned individual commented "You've given it a try; perhaps it's time to explore other avenues". I interpreted this as a form of discouragement, making me doubt the value of my thoughts and feelings. I started to entertain the belief that maybe it was a pursuit I wasn't cut out for, fearing that other people were of the same opinion.

In this case, questioning that belief proved beneficial. Was I allowing this person's remarks to nudge me back into my cage, or was clinging to this belief enabling me to avoid attempting something once more, which truthfully, would require me to embrace vulnerability again, something that was exceptionally uncomfortable the first time around?

Once I admitted that I was letting someone else's narrow-minded perspective limit me and protect my vulnerability, I broke free of that cage and did what I felt was aligned to me and what I value. If I had allowed that comment to tame me, I wouldn't have entered my book for an International Book Award, which it later won. I wouldn't have collaborated on two more books or received ongoing heartfelt messages from people globally who found resonance in my words. Consequently, you wouldn't currently be holding my second book in your hands.

Never be afraid of acting in alignment with who you are and what you value, regardless of the constraints others place on you. This helps to maintain confidence in your choices and opens the cage to unexpected positive outcomes.

SELF AWARENESS CHECK-IN

Where in your life are you being tamed? Who is doing the taming?

CHAPTER FOUR

WHEN LIONS GET CRABS

I have experienced crabs.

And I suspect you have too!

Before you get your tail in a knot, I am, of course, talking about 'Crab Mentality'!

Crab Mentality is a way of thinking best described by the phrase, 'If I can't have it, neither can you'. This phrase was initially coined in the Philippines by writer Ninotchka Rosca, drawing inspiration from the behaviour of crabs confined in a bucket. Put simply, if you have a bucket of crabs, when one crab tries to climb out, the others will pull it back down, preventing any one crab from escaping.

This behaviour has been observed in humans also, where individuals try to undermine or sabotage the success of someone else, particularly when they see that person making progress or achieving their goals. Instead of support, people act out of jealousy, insecurity or competition, trying to ensure that no one else succeeds if they can't.

My first encounter with crabs happened shortly after I published my first book. An experience that pushed me far outside the cozy confines of my comfort zone where previously only a select number of people had insight into the most vulnerable moments of my life. Nevertheless, there was a profound sense of pride for the little book I launched into the world and the positive impact it would bring to others. It seemed like I was finally climbing out of the proverbial bucket I'd felt trapped in for so long, only to find myself pulled back down by an irritating crustacean.

This came in the form of a profoundly intricate letter from someone close to me. Paragraphs of well-crafted and meticulously presented evidence that served as a greatest hits compilation of all the various instances in which I had let this person down. The initial shock rapidly shifted into frustration, anger and hurt, but perhaps the most significant emotion I experienced was a sense of self-righteousness. How dare this person ruin my success by pulling me back down into the bucket with everyone else so I could face my demise.

As I embarked on writing this chapter, the memory of this event was still very fresh in my mind. The hurt and anger took centre stage in my words. Yet, the act of writing my thoughts down and refining them with a different perspective proved to be a powerful tool.

Considering the circumstances surrounding this person at the time the letter manifested, I observed crab mentality in full force. However, the reflection that was designed to pull me back into the bucket also grounded me.

The truth was that the content of this letter wasn't entirely BS. It provided me with the chance to recognise that there were instances when my life was such a hot mess that I couldn't meet the expectations of others, ultimately disappointing them. I, too, have experienced deep dissatisfaction with my own life, during which I became an instigator crab, openly highlighting the flaws in others. It was a reflection of my own unhappiness and in the long run, I was the only one causing harm to myself.

So, whether you are the victim of crabs or the one doing the crabbing, without a level of awareness there is no end to the damage that can be done to yourself or another person. Crab mentality can bring down the fiercest of lions, but only when they are not prepared for it. Below is a guideline for how to detect a crab and prevent yourself from being pulled back into the bucket.

How to Detect a Crab

They . . .

- Possess a fixed mindset, everything is static, there is no room for growth.
- Play small to avoid challenges, they don't venture outside their comfort zone.
- Dislike their current circumstances but aren't willing to change them.
- Compete with everyone, especially those nearest the lip of the bucket.
- Spend most of their time talking about other people rather than their own ideas and solutions.
- Blame everyone else for their shortcomings and accept no responsibility of their own.
- Are candle blowers not candle lighters - they will extinguish your flame rather than ignite it.
- Will never admit they are a crab.

How to Escape the Crabs and Avoid the Bucket

- Establish a growth mindset.
- Play big.
- Change your current circumstances if they don't suit you.
- Focus on collaboration rather than competition
- Lift others up don't pull them down
- Take responsibility for your own shortcomings.
- Ignite the flame in others, don't extinguish them. Be a lion not a crab.
- Change your environment. Climb out of the bucket!

Now that you know a thing or two about crabs and how to escape them, one very important question remains . . .

Are you the one being pulled down or are you the one doing the pulling?

So, what's it going to be? Lion or crab?

P.s. Writing this chapter taught me many lessons, with perhaps the most crucial one being the importance of discretion when entering queries into Google. I can't even begin to describe the results that surfaced when I typed into the search "How to detect a crab"!!!

SELF AWARENESS CHECK-IN

Are you the victim of crabs? When in your life have you been a crab?

CHAPTER FIVE

RAISING CUBS

I'm killing parenthood!

Literally.

Parenthood has been the most profound journey of self-discovery for me. It pushed me deep into adulthood at a pace I wasn't prepared for, to be honest. Yet, there were countless moments when the demands of parenting tested me. It brought me to my knees, filled my thoughts, robbed me of sleep, and instilled a constant fear of stepping away for some much-needed alone time, in case tragedy struck. I've often found myself bewildered, watching these tiny humans wreak havoc on everything I worked hard for, and, at times, I've shamefully questioned why I embarked on this journey in the first place.

Shame. Parenthood is riddled with it. Only to be compounded by those who judge and criticise choices you make, that differ from what they would do for their own children. I've accepted that my parenting style will never be Instagram-worthy and so I have deep admiration and respect for the parents who keep things real by owning the fact they don't always have the answer and realising that parenting is, in equal parts, a science, an art and a shit-show! You'll find that these are the parents who aren't in the business of judging others.

Throughout my Holistic Counselling studies, I gained valuable insights into the intricacies of the human mind. While the knowledge I gained was empowering, there was one particular fact that triggered waves of anxiety in me:

> *"During the first seven years of a child's life, their brain operates in a state of hypnosis, characterised by theta brain waves. During this period, children observe and download all the programming they need to function in life from people, namely parents, around them. They don't question this information; they just take it as fact. It forms a filter on everything and then becomes the lens through which they see the world around them. It becomes their subconscious belief system".*

My first thought after learning this was, "Well, it looks like I've given my kids some prime material for future therapy sessions!"

Thankfully, children never stop learning - that's the reassuring part!

In the year when the entire world faced a pandemic-induced lockdown, one of the first lessons I learnt was how closely my children observed my every move. In times of uncertainty, they looked for my reaction first. They sensed fear in expressions and words, and I learnt very quickly to manage my own fear so I could help them manage theirs. Creating a sense of security is a fundamental human need but by being overly cautious, you can inadvertently disempower a child. Instead, take the opportunity to empower them by transforming their fear into courage. Teaching them that courage is not the absence of fear, but the act of facing it head-on, will be a lasting gift they will carry with them throughout life.

But how can you empower a child if you haven't empowered yourself first?

I firmly believe that one of the most impactful starting points is acknowledging the existence of an 'inner child' within each of us. Deep within you resides your original true self - this is your 'inner child'. During childhood, this authentic self can be wounded when it feels unseen or unheard, an experience common to all of us. This concealed wound can persist into adulthood, influencing how you respond to other people and the challenges that life presents.

In the words of Holistic Psychologist, Nicole LePera, the inner child is the part of your mind that stores all of your emotional experiences from childhood. It serves as a filter through which you view your current experiences as adults. This can impact the choices you make in your relationships, careers and even in your approach to parenting your own children.

Here are three steps you can take towards healing your inner child:

1. Acknowledge you have an inner child
2. Get curious about what triggers your behaviour.
3. Inquire about what it is within you that you need to heal. What wounds are you still carrying from childhood?

As I tried to manage my fear throughout the pandemic, my children taught me the importance of self-healing. I couldn't, in good faith, show up powerfully for them if I hadn't healed my own wounds first. They deserved the gift of an assured, stable and happy mum who wasn't just concerned with raising them but raising them up to be the very best version of themselves.

Regardless of your parental status, it's important to be mindful of how you engage with children. Here are three steps you can take towards helping nurture their inner child:

1. Acknowledge them and their feelings without judgement.
2. Get curious about what triggers their behaviour. For example, are you seeing a disproportionate emotional reaction to something that has happened? Look deeper, what is the underlying emotion or trigger?
3. Inquire about what is going on for them and what they need to heal by really listening, not just to the words, but what they are trying to communicate to you with their behaviour.

One of the most powerful ways we can connect with a child is through emotion. It is not only acceptable for a child to witness your moments of sadness or anger, but it's equally important for them to see you happy and calm as well as how you got there. The key is to show them how to effectively work through tricky emotions, fostering a sense of safety and encouraging them to do the same. Model how you calm yourself, be with them in their difficult moments so you can co-regulate and gradually you will equip them to work through emotions on their own.

Self-awareness is a crucial compass in the journey of parenting or any form of child care-giving. It enables you to recognise your strengths and weaknesses, allowing you to make conscious, informed decisions about how you will go about raising children. By understanding your own emotions, triggers and values, you can respond to children with more empathy and patience. Moreover, self-awareness empowers you to break free from unrealistic expectations and foster a genuine connection with your children, providing them with a nurturing and supportive environment in which to thrive.

SELF AWARENESS CHECK-IN

For those who are parenting right now (e.g. parents, stepparents, foster parents and other carers and many others!)

What is getting in the way of you showing up for your child/ren?

For those who may have children in their lives indirectly (e.g. childcare professionals, aunties and uncles, friends and extended family and many others!)

How can you develop your relationships with children so that you become someone they want to spend time with?

CHAPTER SIX

Purr-fectionism is a Lie

I am a recovering perfectionist.

There really needs to be support groups for this.

A relative of mine enjoys recounting the story of when we first met. Her initial impression of me was that I appeared self-assured and impeccably put together. My clothes, makeup and overall appearance were flawless. Whenever I hear this story, I burst into laughter because it couldn't have been further from the truth.

While it's true that people have their own perceptions, I couldn't help but feel responsible, because the image I was projecting was fraudulent. It was a facade. A big fat lie. Perfectionism became the coping strategy for dealing with my stress, fear and anxiety. If I looked perfect on the outside, then no one would discover how messy I was on the inside. My perfectionism became an exhausting game of constantly needing to prove myself, in order to deter others from noticing my flaws.

Surprisingly, the more 'perfect' I became, the more it seemed to invite scrutiny from others. What hurt the most was when they couldn't find fault with me, they'd turn their attention to my children. When my children suffered because of my need for approval, I knew it was time for a change.

I needed to embrace *Wabi-sabi*.

Wabi-sabi is the Japanese word for finding the hidden beauty in imperfection. What a divine concept!

When I realised that imperfection could possess its own beauty, I embraced the power of vulnerability. The energy I wasted on what others thought started to flow back into my life allowing me to nourish the other things I had neglected while I was so busy projecting my perfect image. Unexpectedly, I discovered that this new-found honesty with myself gave others permission to be honest with me too. It allowed them to drop their defences and for the first time, I started to witness authentic people and conversations. Between us there was no longer a shield constructed by the unattainable images we had designed for ourselves.

Vulnerability connects and binds us as human beings. From the moment we are born we are vulnerable, completely helpless and reliant on those who care for us. We don't have the ability to lie or be anything other than who we are. This creates the strongest bond of all, the bond between parents and their children.

If you hold two pieces of fabric together, the minute you let go, they separate and fall away from each other. But what happens if you attach them with Velcro? They stick. The tiny hooks on one side grasp the tiny loops on the other. They reach out towards each other creating a bond. Vulnerability is basically the 'Velcro' of relationships.

Real connection is not found in the stuff you fabricate. People can only truly connect with the real you. If what they're connecting with is a lie, then you have to continue to upload that unattainable vision.

So don't tell me your life is perfect, tell me it's messy as hell.

Don't tell me that the swimming coach, the soccer coach and the lady who serves your coffee all think your kid is awesome, tell me there are days you struggle to parent them.

Don't walk around with a fake smile on your face, share with me the tears that are sitting behind that smile.

Don't pretend to have your shit together, admit to me that sometimes you don't know who you are or where you are headed.

Don't proclaim to me all your successes, confess to me that you have made mistakes and also failed.

Don't show the world how well you keep it together when faced with challenges or loss, sit with me and fall apart and know that you are not alone.

Tell me that life is hard sometimes.

That things don't work out.

That you have real fears.

That some days there is no light at the end of the tunnel.

That you too wish that you could just escape it all.

If you can unravel in front of me, then I can do it in front of you. You will become my superhero, and we can definitely be friends.

Then you can tell me that as difficult as it can be, tomorrow you will wake up and do it all again because the imperfect warrior inside you truly believes you can, and that same warrior will never again have to do it alone.

SELF AWARENESS CHECK-IN

What imperfections in life do you need to embrace?

CHAPTER SEVEN

Stop Lion to Yourself

I have a highly sensitive BS detector.

I can pick a bullshitter a mile away!

But what's more . . . I can also pick up on the very subtle aromas of my own bullshit too.

This proves invaluable in my line of work. Primarily, my interactions with clients revolve around their belief systems and the emotional pain arising from them. Whether or not they consciously seek help in this area, we always end up delving into it, as their perceptions of the world and themselves are heavily influenced by these beliefs. Notably, a significant number of these perspectives are often incorrect.

One of the initial insights I share with a client in conversations about beliefs is that '*belief*' has the word '*lie*' in it. Sometimes, what you hold to be true about yourself and your environment can be a lie, and the willingness to sit in the discomfort and challenge these beliefs is where the transformative work begins. The aromatic pile of BS you begin to explore is a product of the stories you create about yourself, and the narratives others construct about you.

Numerous discussions with clients have revolved around the idea that external voices can become so ingrained in their self-identity that they lose touch with their own authentic voice. It's no surprise that this leads to dissatisfaction and a life that is disconnected from their true selves.

If you have experienced this, remember that others' views of you are not objective truths; they are simply their personal opinions. You are not defined by these opinions unless you decide to believe them. You are not accountable for how others perceive you, but you do hold responsibility for your own actions.

A client of mine experienced a situation where an individual entered her life through circumstance. This person used manipulation and deceit to influence my client's family into believing certain lies about her, ultimately leading her to adopt those lies as her own internal belief system.

Justifiably, her response was to protect her character, seeking validation from her family. However, upon reflecting on this experience further, we explored the underlying reasons for this reaction. Why did it cause so much distress and why did she need so much validation? This is where things got interesting.

She was able to see the deep unhappiness of the other person reflected in the lies they told. But the anger and hurt that arose from this, possibly stemmed from an initial unwillingness to acknowledge moments in her own past when she might have engaged in similar behaviour towards others.

The most damaging lies are the ones you deceive yourself with. The ego has a way of stepping up to defend you with a sense of entitlement before you have the chance to reflect on your own character. What is important, but often difficult to accept, is that your own lies can eventually catch up with you.

Many people tend to deflect responsibility by insisting that they are not the issue, always attributing fault to others. What truly frustrates me is when someone outright refuses to even entertain the idea that they might play a significant role in their own challenges and circumstances. I can assure you that this mindset will not benefit you in the long run.

The lesson here is to openly listen to others. Identify recurring themes and comments, weigh this information against what you know to be true about yourself, then make a few adjustments if warranted. It may not always be the case that you have a part to play but if you are constantly being met with the same narratives or situations then there comes a point where you need to look at the common denominator . . . you.

Even if you believe your role in an issue is minor, it's worth examining that part. By making even small adjustments to your role, the result can be surprisingly impactful. This approach provides a moment to pause, allowing you to step back before reacting or accepting potential lies as truths.

Acknowledging and taking responsibility for these roles you play doesn't grant you license to be an asshole, as some individuals unfortunately do. On the contrary, you now have awareness and responsibility to catch your BS before it enters the world and negatively affects other people. It's no easy feat to sit and sort through your own garbage, but I have the greatest admiration for people that are brave enough to do so because they are the people who lead the way in helping others reclaim their truth too.

SELF AWARENESS CHECK-IN

What bullshit lies do you keep telling yourself?

CHAPTER EIGHT

Scaredy Cat

My biggest fear is the power of my own fear.

Fear can be a powerful bastard, yet it does serve a significant purpose in your life. Our human design uses fear as its own built-in alarm system. Sometimes fear serves you well by preventing you from dying. But it can also prevent you from living.

When I reflect on my own fear, the words from the song *The Sound of Silence* by Simon and Garfunkel come to mind, *"Hello darkness my old friend. I've come to talk with you again"*.

Fear is like an old friend. It shows up from time to time. It's familiar and you definitely have history together. But it is one of those irritating friends. The kind of friend that, in truth, you've moved on from, but you can't quite shake. The one that keeps showing up in your life from nowhere just when everything seems to be going well to remind you, they're still around.

You're not sure why but maybe, in some twisted way, the way fear makes you feel helps you make sense of your world. Somehow it protects you. When you want to grow, it says, 'slow down'. In times of success, it attributes your achievements to luck. And when change is on the horizon, it tugs on your coattails to anchor you in your comfort zone.

Fear is a thief. It robs you of the joy you might feel, the calm you hope for, and it robs you of what little sanity you have left. It comes in the night when you least expect it, and it greets you first thing in the morning to remind you there are always things to worry about.

Most days, my fear runs the show. It calls the shots. It tells me who's boss and forces me into a corner where I cower and succumb to its relentless message of constant danger and impending doom. It feels like a dirty little secret I carry around with me. The kind of secret that never allows me to truly feel free. I'm too scared to say I'm scared.

Fear has played a prominent role in my life since my dad's passing. I spoke ever so briefly about my personal experience with loss in my previous book *Self Ashored*, but what I failed to communicate was the profound, lingering impact of that loss on my life and the way it gave fear a foothold.

The fear that entrenched itself in my once unshakable existence resembled the ongoing tremors following an earthquake. When I looked at photos of my dad captured a year or two prior to his passing, his exhaustion and weariness were starkly evident. However, during this time, I remained oblivious, engrossed in my own life, and I missed those signs.

I MISSED THE SIGNS.

This is the message my long-time companion, fear, whispered to me every day, as though it were my fault, and I possessed the power to prevent my dad from dying. Before I knew it, fear was insisting that because I couldn't save my dad, I should channel all my energy into preventing similar occurrences. So that's what I did. Everyday became an attempt at world domination in the field of 'life saving'. The challenge was that it created a foundation for potential failure, as I had not only myself to care for but also my husband and children. Each day, fear's grip tightened. The dread of overlooking something crucial in my own children left me feeling paralysed.

The fear became so intense that I found myself unable to function on a daily basis. Instead of taking control of that fear, it took control of me. I became an overbearing mother who resorted to scare tactics, frequent doctor's appointments, blood tests and safe play to make sure no one harboured hidden illnesses, was dying or engaged in activities that would result in death. What kind of a way was that to live? Worse still, what effect was it having on my children? It was only when I saw my fear reflected in their own eyes that I came to the realisation that, among the many things I hoped to impart to them, my fear was not one of them.

The intensity peaked in 2020 amidst a global pandemic. That's the year that I learnt the art of people-watching. I also learnt that if you ever want to witness the worst of human nature, all you have to do is make them afraid.

People-watching is fascinating, but none more so than people-watching online. I watched from the sidelines as everyone in my news feed began expressing their own fears about the state of the world. As time went on, when their fear became too much for them, they projected onto other people. Hoarding toilet paper, howling down anti-vaxxers and abusing shop staff as they did their best to wrestle with supply issues. The thing about fear is that projecting it onto other people doesn't lighten your load, it actually makes it heavier. You become responsible for the collective fear of everyone else. I was watching fear feed the fear in others and it spread faster than any illness.

One of my favourite analogies to illustrate this is the ancient Native American story of the two wolves. A grandfather is speaking to his grandson about an internal battle that happens inside of everyone, the battle between two wolves. One is evil, it represents anger, jealousy, greed, arrogance, sorrow, guilt and ego. The other one is good, it represents joy, peace, love, hope, kindness, compassion and truth. The grandson thinks on this and asks his grandfather "Which wolf wins?". His grandfather replies "The one you feed".

Awareness of your own fear and the tendencies to feed that fear are important. This allows you to have better control over reactions and decisions, ultimately leading to a more balanced existence. Equally important is recognising the impact of your fear on those around you. Understanding how your fear can affect others enables you to be more empathetic, supportive and considerate in your relationships with others.

SELF AWARENESS CHECK-IN

Where is fear taking over your life? How are you projecting this fear onto others?

CHAPTER NINE

FEROCITY

My anger can be volcanic.

It is also a humbling friend.

I came to believe three things about anger growing up: not many people appreciated it, it should be avoided at all costs, and it was bad!

These beliefs stuck with me well into my thirties, even in situations that triggered intense rage. Due to my persistent beliefs about anger, I kept my emotions in check and remained silent. However, as my life became overwhelmed with grief, the anger I bottled up for so long surfaced in a frightening manner. I'm talking full blown, scratch your eyes out, get in my way I'll take you down kind of anger. The most challenging aspect of this feeling was that no one else understood the depth of pain it caused me.

Every morning, I found myself waking up as though I was going into battle, but it was a battle I was fighting on my own. It seemed like everyone around me was carrying on with their lives, and I felt an expectation to do the same. I still had children relying on me, a job requiring my full attention, and a grieving family counting on me. I couldn't afford to acknowledge my anger, and what's more, I didn't know how.

Regrettably, it has become the societal norm that when confronted with difficulties, we should silently endure them and move on. This isn't because it's the most effective way to handle tough situations or manage your emotions, but rather because it's seen as the most beneficial way to spare those around you from excessive discomfort.

By adopting this method, I inadvertently honed my skill for spontaneously combusting over the smallest issue and, in turn, earning labels like "psycho". I've completely lost my composure over the stupidest things, with people observing it unfold, but never seeking to understand why. So, in addition to my already distorted beliefs about anger, I piled on a layer of shame to my emotional burden.

Anger is one of those complex emotions that often carries a negative stigma. It is branded a 'bad emotion' because most of our interaction with it is through aggression. However, there's a distinct difference between someone experiencing anger and channelling it in a healthy manner versus being outworked as aggression leading to hostility, harm and violence. It's no wonder that we are conditioned to believe that suppressing it is the appropriate response.

Anger is a perfectly normal, healthy emotion; the message in anger is one of protection. It is an indication that a boundary has been crossed. It is fuelled by injustice. When properly recognised and expressed, it is an ally that pushes for positive change. Anger can help garner support, shine a light on injustice and encourage self-reflection in others who may be unknowingly fuelling these emotions. It encourages you to create stronger boundaries (more on how to do this in Chapter 15). On the other hand, anger that has been silenced feeds resentment. This is a breeding ground for aggression as we mutter under our breath, undermine others, gossip or become outwardly hostile.

It wasn't until I delved into Karla McLaren's insightful book *The Language of Emotions*, that I discovered the art of befriending my anger. Her book not only provided guidance on how to embrace my anger but also granted me the freedom to express it without any sense of shame. I began to understand just how multi-layered my anger was. My grief was not the catalyst for my volcanic anger; rather it acted as an amplifier for what was already simmering away within me - the pain from past experiences where I remained silent. Learning to honour my anger by giving it a voice allowed me to listen to its message. It revealed the areas of my life where I needed to establish stronger boundaries and those that were in need of healing, as the anger from words I never spoke became the thorns in my side.

Plucking at the thorns one by one, I have replaced my old faulty beliefs about anger that did not serve me. The three things I now believe are: it needs to be honoured, its message is one of protection and boundaries, and a punching bag is your best friend.

Let me end this chapter by sharing a fable called Androcles and the Lion.

Androcles was a slave who was mistreated by his master. One day he decided to escape and found refuge in a nearby forest. As he was searching for a safe place to sleep for the night, he came face to face with a lion roaring with incredible ferocity. Certain he was to be the lion's next meal, Androcles turned to flee the beast but was halted by the glistening tears and sadness in the lion's eyes. Instead of running, Androcles approached the lion with caution. As he got nearer, he noticed that deeply embedded within his paw was a thorn. The lion wasn't seeking to maliciously attack Androcles, he was in extreme pain.

Androcles extended his arm slowly, gently stroked the lion's mane and reassured him as he extracted the thorn from his paw and bound it in cloth. The lion licked his face, and they became friends for life.

Rushing to pass judgement on others can cause you to miss opportunities for kindness. Consider the origins of someone else's anger and what they may be attempting to convey. On the other hand, when we lack understanding of our own anger and are not willing to receive help from others, that's when it can become toxic. The pain you carry may be so deeply ingrained within your body that it simmers away until the smallest thing causes it to overflow.

Becoming better acquainted with your anger is largely attributed to better understanding your 'thorns' and speaking the truth about it to other people without the ferocity. When we tend to our own wounds first, it allows us the grace to understand the thorns of others.

SELF AWARENESS CHECK-IN

What thorns are you concealing? How can you deal with your anger assertively?

CHAPTER TEN

Licking Your Wounds

I used to be an 'ice-skater'.

I use the term 'ice-skater' very loosely because let's face it my friend, I spent more time on my ass than I did on my feet!

My mum enrolled me in ice-skating lessons when I was quite young, with only one goal in mind: she thought it would be something fun I could do with my friends one day. She never expected me to become a world champion figure skater, nor did she expect that I would continue with lessons for as long as I did, considering I spent my very first lesson crying and refusing to move from the barrier because the instructor terrified me.

The day I turned sixteen, I was set to compete with my ice-skating Precision team at Nationals in Perth (think synchronised swimming but on ice). The competition consisted of two routines, a short program and a long program. I was the reserve for the long program, which spoke volumes about my ability level! I was quietly relieved though, because the intricacies of the long program triggered my anxiety!

As fate would have it, one of our strongest skaters suffered an injury during the short program, and you guessed it, plans were in motion for me to skate in her place.

Our team manager sat me down and gently asked how I felt about skating. While I expressed my desire to throw up, I believed I could do it and was absolutely determined not to let my team down. On the contrary, our team coach didn't share the same belief in my abilities. I can still vividly recall her pacing back and forth in the room, which oddly enough induced more anxiety in me than the prospect of skating the long program. It was clear that her belief in our injured skater far exceeded her belief in me and come hell or high water, she was going to skate. It was never communicated to me that I could also undertake the challenge and do it well.

The unspoken words I internalised from that exchange were, "You will fail, you will let the team down, you're not good enough". Thus began the internal monologue that permeated other areas of my life for years to come. I never ended up skating the long program, I also never returned to the ice after that competition.

I am a self-professed high achiever. Failure is not a word that appears often in my vocabulary. Anything I set my mind to I am determined to master and complete. I don't give up easily, if at all, but if you were to ask me to name one thing I truly felt I failed at, the unequivocal answer would be ice-skating every time. My dream of landing a triple axel was shattered in a split second because I allowed someone else to define failure for me.

For twenty-four years, I carried a deep sense of resentment toward that entire experience until I read Marie Forleo's book, *Everything is Figureoutable* where she wrote, "I win, or I learn but I never fail". This greatly shifted my perspective on failure, ultimately fostering a level of self-awareness where I no longer felt compelled to excel in everything I do. Now, when I revisit that experience, I do so with a heart full of gratitude instead of bitterness. At the very least, I can appreciate that I can not only support myself on the ice but also my children. It's something we can do for fun, just as my mum had intended. I don't shy away from sharing that 'failure' with them without shame. At most, my coach served as a prime example of what I did not wish to become.

It's not by chance that I found myself in a profession where my primary mission is to instil belief in others. As a transformational coach, I have the privilege of providing individuals with what I once yearned for so deeply. I guide them in challenging the self-imposed narratives they tell themselves. I support them in approaching both failure and success with gratitude and a genuine thirst for learning. I assist them in embracing the value of their life's journey thus far and set a direction for the future. Above all, I have the honour of walking alongside them as they succeed in realising their dreams.

The wounds that were inflicted on me all those years ago weren't physical; they were to my pride, ego and self-esteem. Inwardly, I felt a profound hurt, transforming me from a determined teen to a cautious and compliant woman in my twenties and thirties. It took me quite some time to address and tend to the wounds of my own soul, but it gave me the opportunity to support my son through his first significant setback.

Toby had a multimedia assessment to complete with a partner, but due to time limitations and illness, the task couldn't be completed to its full potential. He approached Stuart and me, in tears, admitting devastation over his first ever fail grade. We had a brief moment to reframe his perception of failure. Stuart and I exchanged glances, shared a high-five, and reassured Toby that this was terrific news. The poor kid thought he'd entered the Twilight Zone, and his parents had gone completely insane.

It was in that moment that he grasped the worth of failure. He recognised it was nothing to loathe, hate or fear. In that moment, failure became his friend. With the right reaction and a few kind words of support, he knew everything was going to be okay. His fear, anxiety and sadness soon passed, allowing him to learn the lessons on offer. Nowadays, he rationalises everything, especially setbacks. He made himself vulnerable to failure but wide-open to learning.

Don't give up just because things unfold differently than you envisioned. The first failure is always the hardest and this is often what will defeat you. Don't let it. In the words of Billie Jean King, it's not failure; it's research. Get comfortable with failing but fail well. What I'm getting at is, look for the lessons. Like a researcher, get curious about what went wrong, what you could change, but more importantly, what you did right. Pick yourself up, dust yourself off, lick your wounds, make necessary adjustments and give it another shot.

SELF AWARENESS CHECK-IN

What failures of yours have become lessons?

CHAPTER ELEVEN

LION-HEARTED

I struggle to forgive some people.

To be honest, it is the thing I battle with the most.

I have pondered this conundrum for years. Can I forgive and forget? Do I truly forgive if I can't forget? Am I even capable of forgiveness?

Forgiveness is the ability to recall what has happened without the pain and hurt. If you can achieve this, you have experienced true forgiveness. It's a word that gets thrown around a lot, like it's the easiest thing in the world to do. I've even found myself saying it to my own children, "Just forgive each other and move on". However, I have come to understand that it's rarely as straightforward as that. As it turns out, forgiving is really challenging.

Regrettably, what many people define as forgiveness often amounts to mere words or a state of limbo where the pain has dulled but lingers, waiting for the right moment to resurface when you're most vulnerable. A valuable lesson I've gained from my own journey is that forgiveness is not a single event, it's a process. You need to allow yourself the time to work through the hurt and pain and, as you do, the grace to forgive will emerge bringing with it a certain amount of peace.

When I started to reflect on the trouble I was having with forgiveness, I couldn't find the grace and peace I knew I needed. I told myself I had forgiven but every time I recalled the situation in question, the pain was there, lessened perhaps but still there, clear as day. I found myself asking what it was I was truly not forgiving. Was it other people and their actions and words, or was it myself?

I must admit that this chapter has been one of the most challenging to write. There were many times I wrote a paragraph and deleted it because it was just full of anger and that is not the energy I wanted to convey. So, I took myself outside, sat with the warm Autumn sun on my back and tuned in to what my heart had to say. The insights were profound. I started to reflect on the times I had inflicted pain and hurt on others and there were plenty of occasions to consider! All at once, it occurred to me how hypocritical it would be for me to claim that I had forgiven someone else, when I hadn't even forgiven myself.

Self-forgiveness is one of the hardest things to do, but it is fundamental and necessary for personal growth and inner peace. The path to self-forgiveness requires acknowledging your own mistakes, understanding that those mistakes are redeemable and accepting that you are not a perfect human. Forgiveness frees you and not forgiving keeps you stuck in anger and pain.

Through this self-reflection, you gain the capacity to extend forgiveness to others as you come to realise your own moments of imperfection that are equally deserving of forgiveness. Achieving a state of true forgiveness begins with a willingness to forgive in another person that which you are willing to forgive in yourself. It isn't about condoning past actions, and you are not obliged to forget them. From a scientific standpoint it's a formidable task when emotions are involved. Forgiveness, at its core, is the art of letting go.

A brilliant analogy that illustrates this well is to imagine yourself gripping onto a rope, much like in a tug-of-war. You firmly hold one end while a person or past event that has caused you pain, anger, resentment and hurt pulls on the other end. You exert significant effort to maintain your grip on that rope because you don't want to grant them the satisfaction of your forgiveness. However, the paradox lies in the fact that by clinging to the rope too tightly, you eventually end up with rope burn. Recognising when to release your grip and free yourself from the hold of that person or event is pivotal. If you don't let it go, it results in more harm than good.

Forgiveness involves a decision to lessen the grip. It requires a truck load of courage and the ability to dig deep into your soul. Forgiveness is a position of strength, it is not giving up or giving in, it's letting yourself off the hook and that's a powerful step. Nothing has stronger healing power than forgiveness. Perhaps if, like me, you are willing to forgive yourself for the mistakes you have made, for the people you have hurt and for the integrity you have lost, it will allow you the grace to forgive that in others too.

SELF AWARENESS CHECK-IN

What do you need to forgive yourself for?

PART TWO

Self-Acceptance

Own Yourself

What changes do you need to make to align with who you want to be?

Now that you have begun to develop an awareness of who you are, it's time to learn how to embrace it. This part is about accepting all of you. The way to do this is to explore areas of your life where you haven't been living in alignment with your core values. Humans have a beautiful duality - a light and shadow side, our good qualities and flaws. In order to wholly love, respect and accept who you are you need to learn to explore and nurture both sides. Life is not just about loving the good parts; it's owning and accepting that the shadow side needs just as much love and attention. In this section you'll discover just how to do this. Each chapter concludes with a short exercise and alignment affirmation to repeat to assist you in accepting even the most uncomfortable aspects of who you are.

CHAPTER TWELVE

The Hunt

My core values are my moral compass.

They keep me aligned.

Your core values guide your decision making, they shape your intentions, drive your actions and help to define your priorities. Your life mirrors these values, so having clarity on them is essential for living authentically and powerfully. As self-awareness deepens, your core values become increasingly evident.

Frequently though, I observe individuals diminish the importance of their core values out of apprehension, fearing personal attacks or criticism. However, a crucial first step towards self-acceptance lies in acknowledging and embracing your core values. These values are intrinsic to your personal identity and accepting them is the foundation for living authentically. By cultivating a genuine acceptance of these values, you can begin to foster a stronger sense of self that is unshaken by external judgement.

To fully harness the advantages of aligning with your core values, it's essential to delve into them and actively amplify their presence in your daily life. For instance, as family holds a central place among my core values, I invest time and energy into nurturing those relationships. This action makes aspects of my life less demanding, as I immerse myself in activities that I love and that bring me joy. The synergy between my actions and values amplifies the benefits not only for myself but also for my family. Conversely, directing time and energy towards areas misaligned with my core values results in more effort for less impact.

If you don't know what you value or what you stand for, you don't know where to expend your effort in a way that will not only bring you joy but will have the greatest impact on yourself and others.

The way to begin living an amplified life is to go on the hunt for your core values by following the steps below:

Identify Your Core Values

Step 1
From the list below mark or highlight all the core values that resonate with you. Don't overthink it. If you think of a value not on the list add it in.

Step 2
Take the words from Step 1 and rank them in importance based on where your life is right now. List your top 3 below:

My Top 3 Core Values

1.
2.
3.

Core Values List

Abundance	Health	Love
Accomplishment	Honesty	Loyalty
Authenticity	Inner Harmony	Making a Difference
Bravery	Inspiration	Nature
Compassion	Integrity	Personal Growth
Connection	Joy	Security
Creativity	Justice	Self-Respect
Experiences	Kindness	Spirituality
Family	Knowledge	Trust
Freedom	Leadership	Wisdom
Generosity	Life Balance	Zest for Life

Step 3

Add an action to each value so you can see what it looks like e.g. If my top value is 'Making a Difference', I might add 'Seek opportunities' and end up with **Seek opportunities to make a difference.** This now is a clear, actionable goal that you can implement in order to amplify the way that you are living and to align more closely to your values.

Examples of Actions

- Seek opportunities to . . .
- Live with more . . .
- Be more . . .
- Learn more about . . .
- Educate myself on . . .
- Practise . . .
- Develop . . .
- Share . . .
- Demonstrate . . .
- Nurture . . .

Step 4

Print out your core values and make them visible to you every day.

ALIGNMENT AFFIRMATION

I allow my inner guide to show me the way.

CHAPTER THIRTEEN

Lion and Lioness

Marriage has kicked my ass.

One of the most magical things about self-acceptance is that it teaches you to see where other people are at in their life and be patient with what you see. This grants you the opportunity to accept other people for who they are and not seek to change them. My marriage to Stuart has been the most influential guide in developing this understanding. Over twenty years of partnership has seen the good, the bad and the downright ugly sides of both our personalities. We entered into marriage with a 'We've totally got this' attitude.

We totally didn't.

Our perception of a mature and highly functional relationship turned out to be an illusion when we discovered that neither one of us knew how to effectively handle conflict. Our values as individuals didn't match up with our values as a couple and because communication skills were still developing, conflict ensued.

Let's be clear; I genuinely believe there's no one else in the world who could tolerate my shit the way my husband does.

I don't know anyone with enough patience and love to embrace my fifty personalities and Stuart S.J. Pearson is undoubtedly my biggest supporter. However, it's also a fact that the man has a unique talent for pushing every single one of my buttons. It's quite a gift, to be honest!

Following a particularly challenging moment, I vividly remember tuning into a television interview featuring a celebrity couple a few years into their seemingly perfect marriage. They boldly asserted that they had never had an argument. In response, I couldn't help but yell at the television 'Liars!". Either that or they are both suppressing significant aspects of themselves and their true desires, fearing it would shatter the illusion of their blissful marriage. The media portrayed their relationship as an ideal to strive for.

In any relationship, irrespective of its nature, conflict will arise. Defining a happy relationship as one that is free of conflict is both unhelpful and unrealistic, as it overlooks the essential role of communication and growth in fostering meaningful connections. Let me emphasise that I am referring to conflict, not violence, there are very distinct differences. Conflict arises when a person doesn't feel seen, heard or accepted. It happens when values and viewpoints don't align. Handled well, conflict is healthy. It signals a need for something to change. If there is no conflict or differing opinion, how could you ever grow as an individual or as a couple? Conflict strengthens your ability to face challenges that arise and trust me when I tell you, no matter how magical a relationship seems, challenges will arise and arise in abundance.

As a society we need to let go of the illusion that a perfect relationship exists. We need to move past the notion that any indication of conflict signals impending doom. We need to understand that a relationship grows and changes as you and your partner grow and change. This also means that what you both value individually and as a couple will change. Stuart and I haven't stayed married to the person we first fell in love with. We have stayed married to ten different versions of that person as we grew. We learnt how to elevate each other rather than push each other's buttons. We learnt to find where our values fit together and learnt to respect where they differ. But most importantly, we have witnessed each other's magic and learnt to remind each other of that magic when we have forgotten.

As you continue to move through the pages of this book you will soon realise that one of the most powerful ways to improve your relationships with others is to improve the relationship you have with yourself first.

If you are in a partnership, engaging in the following two activities can aid in understanding and accepting the values that matter both individually and as a couple. If you're unpartnered, focus on cultivating a strong relationship with yourself by incorporating some of these rituals in daily life and nurturing connections with friends and family.

Create Shared Rituals

American Psychologist, John Gottman, has worked for over four decades in the field of marriage stability and divorce prediction. In his best-selling book *The Seven Principles for Making Marriage Work*, Gottman shares concepts, behaviours and skills that can have a positive impact on long-lasting relationships.

His seventh principle - Create Shared Meaning - is something I can attest to. An important goal of any relationship is fostering an environment where each person feels encouraged to express their aspirations openly. The more genuine and respectful conversations you have, the greater the likelihood of discovering shared meaning. The concept of creating rituals has played a pivotal role in my own marriage. A ritual we have maintained from the beginning is our Saturday night date night. While we may not always go out, we intentionally set aside time for just the two of us to enjoy takeout, watch a movie, or engage in conversation over a glass of wine and a shared plate of nibbles. It is something we look forward to in our week providing us with the opportunity to connect, dream, plan, discuss and problem-solve together.

In his book *Wired for Love*, couple's therapist, Stan Tatkin, also speaks of the importance of creating rituals. He found that couples who make plans to meet each other in bed at night and routinely wake together in the morning, report more relationship satisfaction than couples who sleep and wake separately. He suggests implementing a week of ritual. This can be such a fun and lovely way of connecting with your partner.

Set a week aside and implement some of the rituals from the list below.

- Go to bed together.
- Wake up together.
- Make breakfast in bed.
- Kiss when you wake up and before you go to bed.
- Have a daily debrief.
- Read a book together.
- Listen to music over a glass of wine.
- Have a date night.
- Make time to make love.
- If you have children, work together to put the children to bed.
- Watch a show together with a cup of tea after kids have gone to bed.
- Have some separate time.

- Introduce an element of surprise.
- Cook dinner together.
- Have a welcome home ritual.

At the end of the week, discuss how a week of rituals made you feel. What did you like? What didn't quite work? Did you notice any change in each other?

How To Uplift Your Partner

Another great exercise Tatkin suggests is particularly useful for when conflict arises. It helps respective partners know what to do to help or diffuse a situation. It is essentially about becoming an expert on your partner.

What are the things you can say or do that have the power to shift and elevate your partner's mood or state of being?

1. Know each other's vulnerabilities e.g. one of mine is that what I do for my children is never enough.
2. Use words of affirmation e.g. If Stuart were to notice I was down on myself for not doing enough, he could point out all the things I have done for my children that have benefitted them.
3. Write a list for each other of the things the other can say or do that will help to diffuse conflict e.g. One that works for me is when Stuart tells me to go take a breather and he will make me a cup of tea and then come and sit with me for a chat.
4. Sit and compare notes over a wine or romantic dinner (ritual).

ALIGNMENT AFFIRMATION

I am worthy of a healthy, supportive, loving relationship.

CHAPTER FOURTEEN

Your Pride

I am naturally introverted.

Not your typical Leo trait.

Leo personalities lean more towards extroversion, and they enjoy being centre stage. Much like lions themselves, who are the most sociable of the big cats. Lions are also the only cat species that live in a group known as a 'pride'. Prides can be as small as 3 or as big as 40 lions, the average is about 15. Within each pride, every lion has a role. The hunting and cub-rearing is generally carried out by the females while the males defend their territory.

Human society is much the same. We are wired for connection. Without it, the world can be a very lonely and hostile place in which to live. To traverse the terrain of your life you need a strong 'pride' around you - your tribe, your circle, your people. To me, this is not about finding the people who will be part of your life forever. It's more about finding the people who will impact your life in a powerful way. These people might not stick around for long, but their presence changes the trajectory of your life. These are the people who are around to challenge you to think differently. They are the people who you crave conversation with. They are the ones who accompany you to the next stage of your beautiful existence.

In recent years, my introversion has resulted in fewer close connections, yet the quality of those connections has significantly increased in value. My 'pride' consists of eight very honourable roles that are filled by individuals who bring something unique to the group. Each possesses an important quality of equal value that, together, helps me flourish and become a better human. My pride feeds my soul and these special people know I love them fiercely even when I can't physically give of myself as often as they would like.

I've identified eight fundamental traits within my pride. I've playfully assigned names that truly encapsulate their essence and significance. This dynamic isn't a one-way street; in the best prides, each member contributes to the collective, and together, they form a synergy where the whole is undoubtedly greater than the sum of its parts. The eight personalities in my pride are:

1. Grounded Grace - she keeps things real and balanced. She helps to explore things from all angles and is a rock in difficult situations.
2. Wild Willow - fun and adventurous, she appeals to your wild side. Her childlike sense of wonder compels you to try new things and explore new places you wouldn't have otherwise considered.
3. Kick-Ass Kim - she is full of energy and zest for life. Her enthusiasm makes things happen. She wants to see you succeed and helps you do so with her signature kick-ass attitude and go get 'em spirit.

4. Nurturing Natalie - like a big warm blanket and cup of tea, she brings all things love and comfort to your life. She is your safe space to stop and take care of your soul so you can replenish your strength to face life head on.
5. Challenging Charli - she pushes you outside your comfort zone and challenges your thoughts and beliefs about life. She will turn everything on its head but without her you will never know what you are capable of. Her belief in you is unwavering.
6. Supportive Suzy - Your biggest cheerleader. She is always there to celebrate your biggest wins and hold your hand through the losses. Ready to offer an emergency glass of wine or cup of tea, constant support and encouragement, even of your craziest pursuits. Be sure never to take her for granted.
7. Soulful Sage - Sage by name, sage by nature. She is your well of wisdom and spiritual guidance. Time and again she will connect you back to the truth of who you are.
8. Visionary Veronique - Your big picture person. She ignites the fire within you that tends to silently flicker away. She makes you feel anything is possible.

Now your turn - who fills these roles within your pride (it doesn't matter if you can't fill in one person for each, set the intention for them to show up at the right time)? You can add any other's you think of or change the names or gender - it's your pride! The roles you need are entirely up to you!

1. Grounded Grace:
2. Wild Willow:
3. Kick-Ass Kim:
4. Nurturing Natalie:

5. Challenging Charli:
6. Supportive Suzy:
7. Soulful Sage:
8. Visionary Veronique:

ALIGNMENT AFFIRMATION

I am making room for amazing people to enter my life.

CHAPTER FIFTEEN

Marking Your Territory

If you cross a boundary, I will call you on it.

One of my favourite quotes on boundaries comes from Najwa Zebian - "Boundaries are not about what you are protecting yourself from. They are about what you are protecting within yourself".

Setting boundaries is necessary for mental health and wellbeing. Boundaries are personal limits you set for yourself, not for other people. They are your way of communicating what you are willing to accept and what you are not.

Setting and maintaining boundaries was never my strong suit. I tended to be overly forgiving towards those who took advantage of my lack of boundaries, earning myself the label of a people pleaser. This inadvertently communicated that this was acceptable and would go without consequences.

It wasn't until my thirties, that I came to a profound realisation about the substantial impact my lack of boundaries had on my overall wellbeing. In realising that I was the sole architect of my boundaries and only I could enforce them, I was able to assertively establish limits and reclaim control in various aspects of my life. As I consistently upheld these boundaries, a transformative shift occurred - those around me began to understand and respect these newfound limits, creating a healthier and more empowered dynamic in my relationships with others.

Have you ever felt that your lack of boundaries has been taken advantage of?

The most resentful and stressed people in the world have no boundaries. Usually because they have spent a good chunk of their life doing things for others under sufferance or obligation or being 'talked into' things because they stayed silent. Sitting with resentment without appropriately voicing how you feel drives a wedge between yourself and others. Disconnection breeds in the absence of communication. People are not mind-readers and will often be left perplexed when you suddenly decide not to talk to them anymore. When you set boundaries and communicate them, people know what to expect from you. You can easily say yes and no to things, stand by your decision and not feel guilty.

The great American writer and mythologist, Joseph Campbell, said that for something to be sacred, draw a circle around it. Everything inside that circle is sacred. It is a line that no one can cross. It is your boundary.

What do you need to keep sacred? Your time? Your energy? Your privacy? What do you need to protect within yourself? Your peace? Your self-belief? Your integrity?

Once you start to set firm, clear boundaries, I can almost guarantee you that there will be push-back from those who are not used to you having any. This is temporary and it means it's working! Change is uncomfortable but the small amount of discomfort you may feel from setting boundaries will save you years of anger and resentment, not to mention saving relationships in the process. And it goes without saying that one of the best ways to help people respect your boundaries, is for you to respect theirs in return.

How to Set Healthy Boundaries in 3 Easy Steps

1. Define it.
2. Communicate it.
3. Stick to it.

Define It - state clearly what you want! Take a good look at where you are lacking boundaries (Hint: usually in areas where people tend to piss you off the most e.g. relationships, work, Christmas time etc)

Communicate It - people are not mind readers. Therefore, you cannot expect people to know what your boundaries are unless you communicate them - assertively not aggressively. Don't be afraid to say no. The best part is that you don't have to have a reason either. Justifying your boundaries weakens them - it comes across like you're apologising for having enough courage to say what you do (and don't) want.

Stick To It - if you don't stick to it then it becomes a suggestion rather than a boundary. Will it be difficult? Umm yes! Especially when you receive push back from other people who are inconvenienced by your boundary. But let me put it this way, if you don't stick to your boundaries, in the long run, will it be more uncomfortable for you or for them? It's like sticking to any other habit, after a certain time it will just become a normal, accepted part of everyday living.

I have identified eight areas where you need to get very clear on the boundaries that need to be in place:

1. Time - how much of your time are you willing to give?
2. Personal Space - your body, your rules. Kissing? Hugging?
3. Health - what will you and won't you feed your body?
4. Conversation - what topics are you comfortable discussing or not discussing?
5. Emotional - how much emotional energy are you willing to take on board from other people?
6. Sexual - consent is 100% yours. Are you willing to discuss what pleases you and what doesn't?
7. Intellectual - what opinions and beliefs do you hold?
8. Material - how will you spend money? What are you willing to share with others?

Here are some of mine:

- I will limit the time and energy I spend on people who drain me.
- I will say no when I physically, emotionally or mentally feel exhausted.
- I will exit any conversation I am not comfortable contributing to.
- I will not tolerate any disrespectful behaviour or words directed at me or my children and will intervene to safeguard their boundaries where they can't do so themselves.
- I will have a brave conversation with people that have crossed a boundary.
- I will no longer interact with people who consistently cross these boundaries.

Reflect on the following areas and define the boundary you need to create:

1. Time -
2. Personal Space -
3. Health -
4. Conversation -
5. Emotional -
6. Sexual -
7. Intellectual -
8. Material -

ALIGNMENT AFFIRMATION

Every day I become clearer about the boundaries that serve me best.

CHAPTER SIXTEEN

BE COMFORTABLE IN YOUR OWN FUR

I'm not always comfortable with who I am.

I too have moments of 'not enough-ness', of body shaming myself and 'comparison-itis'.

I too find myself entangled in the constant stream of images and products on social media, catering to the idealised body type. This leads me down a confusing path of distorted information about carbs, calories, sugars, strategies for perkier boobs and exercises to counteract the effects of the three doughnuts I enjoyed for breakfast. I can't even begin to tell you the money I have wasted on products to make things stop sagging, wrinkling, wobbling or hurting. In the end, all of this only reinforced the harmful message that my efforts are not enough, my body is not enough and I'm not enough.

The challenging yet grounding reality is that at forty-something years of age, my body no longer resembles my twenty-year-old self, not even close. Honestly, considering what it has been through, how could I expect otherwise? Six surgeries, three of them births, why would I have nothing but deep admiration and gratitude for what my body has endured?

Here's the reason: too much conversation focuses on what's going wrong in our minds and bodies, fixating on comparing rather than complimenting. Shifting towards healthier, well-rounded wellbeing messaging is crucial, along with greater appreciation for what our bodies already do for us.

Rather than focusing on admiring someone's toned appearance in their new activewear or the swift post-birth body recovery, let's celebrate the bodies bravely fighting chronic illness every day. What about those remarkable bodies sustaining through the process of growing and delivering a tiny human? Or those enduring numerous heart-wrenching procedures in the quest to conceive?

When are we ever going to learn that the vessel that houses all the vital organs to keep us alive, that allows us to sit and stand and run and digest food, that breathes and processes deep emotions, is already doing enough?

What captivates me most in a person isn't their gym attendance, a diet of green smoothies, or a specific weight. It's the beauty of someone comfortable in their own skin, courageously embracing their body with all its strengths and flaws. A person unbothered by size, feeling deeply and passionately, confidently expressing that they love, accept and respect themselves exactly as they are.

If you are going to embrace and accept all of you then you can't just pick and choose the parts you are most comfortable with and neglect the rest. In order to sit with the parts that are not so desirable and accept them as part of the beautiful tapestry that is your life, there needs to be a level of discomfort you will need to work through.

All the battle wounds you carry both externally and internally need love and compassion. The wisdom and clarity that can be gleaned from those wounds is astounding - about who you are, what you stand for and what a miracle your living, breathing body is. This wisdom begins with learning to only ever seek validation from yourself. No one else determines your worth because no one else sees who you truly are.

'Living your best life' does not come from what you wear, what you eat, how much money you earn or being able to pretzel yourself into what society believes is 'enough'. Your best life comes from the authentic way you show up for yourself and embrace yourself - flaws and all. It is only then that you can truly grow and transform as you should.

Write a Personal Manifesto

A personal manifesto boldly affirms your acceptance of individuality, declares how you'll support and love yourself, and outlines the contribution you aspire to make to the world.

Examples of statements you could use:

> I believe . . .
> I will . . .
> I love . . .
> I am committed to . . .
> I want to live in a world that . . .
> I know this to be true . . .

It may look like this:

> I believe in the power of authenticity.
> I will cultivate self-love by acknowledging my strengths and learning from my flaws.

I love the pursuit of knowledge knowing that growth comes from curiosity and an open mind.

I am committed to uplifting others and celebrating our differences and shared humanity.

I want to live in a world that values kindness, empathy and diversity.

I know this to be true: Every moment is a chance to choose kindness.

Steps for Writing

1. Be inspired by other manifestos.
2. Write down some statements using the above examples.
3. Write a first draft.
4. Sit on it for a few days.
5. Re-read it and make any necessary adjustments.
6. As you read it pay attention to how it feels in your body. Does it stir emotion?
7. Make any final adjustments.
8. Live it.

ALIGNMENT AFFIRMATION

I choose my own definition of what it means to be enough.

CHAPTER SEVENTEEN

Purr-poseful Intentions

I am intentional with my words and actions.

But, like all humans, when I lose my way, those words and actions are not always carried out with the best of intentions. When someone has hurt me, said or done the wrong thing or spread lies, my instinctive reaction is to want to get even and right the wrong. My need to be heard is driven by my survival instincts. These instincts seek to protect and prevent me from being socially ostracized. As a result, my ability to act consciously is diminished and my words and actions are dictated by the stress response. I become far removed from my authentic, intentional self. I end up sabotaging my progress towards my goals, hurting other people, and also hurting myself in the process.

Living an intentional life means what I do, what I say and how I show up for people is aligned and serves a purpose. When I am at my best, making choices mindfully and not out of fear, anger or stress, I get vastly better results. And, what's more, I'm making progress towards my goals.

Bear in mind though, that there is a distinct difference between intentions and goals. Goals have a destination in mind. Once you have reached that destination, you choose another goal. An intention, on the other hand, is the reason behind your actions.

Having clarity about your reasons allows you to choose different paths along the way and reassess your actions if you find they are straying from the goal and misaligned with your original intention. Intentions are the roadmap to the destination that keeps you in touch with who you are and what you want to achieve. You know your intentions are aligned when the choices you make are conscious and deliberate rather than subconscious and automatic. Every choice you make either supports or undermines your intention.

Having clear intentions is often more important than the actual outcome. When you are living an intentional life, the learning and personal growth along your journey are exactly what you need to clarify and refine (or completely change) your goals. You will likely find new perspectives and develop new skills that may render your original goals irrelevant.

So how do you live intentionally?

It all comes back to how much you love and accept yourself exactly as you are. If you don't truly love and accept yourself then it will almost certainly show up in the intentions behind your words and actions. You need to be consistently working on your self-awareness and self-acceptance and guard against self-criticism, poor self-talk and perfectionism if you are to live intentionally.

In a practical sense, living intentionally also requires you to choose your battles. One of my hardest-won lessons in life is that, in the face of injustice, I don't always need to be vocal about it. Sometimes, if my intentions are honourable, I just need to let my actions speak for themselves.

In my experience, your intentions will be most challenged and exposed in the following situations:

- Social media - What is your intention for posting? Why are you commenting?
- Career Choices - Why is this choice important or desirable to you? How do you show up each day at your workplace?
- Relationships - What is it that you value in this relationship/friendship? What compromises are you willing (or not willing) to make?
- Spiritual life - What is it that you believe? How do you live this out?

When you set intentions that align with your true self, here are some key questions to help you remain mindful in your decision-making:

Why am I doing this?
Is what I am about to say or do coming from a place of love or fear?
Is what I am about to say or do an act of kindness?
Is what I am about to say or do align with my values?
Is what I am about to say or do a true reflection of who I am?

Becoming more intentional takes practice and commitment. Adopt small changes in one part of your life and, as your success increases, broaden this to other parts of your life. In this way you begin to live in alignment with who you truly are, and this will become evident in all you say and do.

Create a Sankalpa (the yogic practice of intention setting)

San = higher or highest sense of truth
Kalpa = a vow

What you will be creating here is a vow to support your highest truth.

Begin by sitting in a quiet space - at home or in nature. Create stillness in your body by gently closing your eyes if you feel comfortable to do so and take three slow, deep breaths. Take a moment to pay attention to the rise and fall of your breath, allowing any unhelpful thoughts to come and go without engaging in them. Spend some time reflecting on the following questions:

- What do I truly want for my life?
- In what areas of my life am I not aligned with this?
- What changes can I make to align with this intention?

Following the five steps below, create a sankalpa that reflects the answers to these questions.

1. Make your intention about you.
2. Tune into how it feels in your body.
3. State your intention positively and in the present tense.
4. Keep in simple.
5. Live it.

Some examples:

I work to create justice in the world.
I listen to learn and understand.

My voice is worthy of being heard.
I treat myself with love and compassion.

ALIGNMENT AFFIRMATION

My intentions are honourable and serve the highest good.

CHAPTER EIGHTEEN

The Lion Sleeps Tonight

I love solitude.

It energises me. But no one can be alone all the time, there needs to be a healthy balance.

Lions can't be on the hunt all the time; they will burn out. Rest is a priority, and energy needs to be conserved if they are to be effective and successful hunters.

The same priorities need to be applied to humans. But resting or, dare I say, 'self-care' has become a frivolous word that tends to imply luxury rather than what it truly means. Self-care is a fundamental honouring, grounding and reconnection practice that replenishes the core of who you are.

This chapter is perhaps the most important chapter in the whole book and my hope is that it will have an influential role in your self-acceptance. You can work through your "bullshit", you can identify your values, you can align your goals, but all this will mean sweet bugger all if your mind, body and soul aren't in alignment with one another. The only way for this to happen is through commitment to honouring yourself.

I know straight away when I have neglected myself for too long; I get fatigued, resentful, angry, my body starts to yell at me through pain and in my heart and mind every single thing that has ever pissed me off resurfaces. But I don't rest because, like most women, I am an expert at self-criticism and guilt when I even contemplate self-care. It's selfish, right? But when is it acceptable to be selfish?

There was a moment in my life I realised something needed to change. I just could not sustain the level of neglect I realised I had inflicted on myself. I began to resemble the wicked witch from *The Wizard of Oz* in the scene when she's melting. Everything about me felt like it was disintegrating - mind, body and soul.

It was my 40th trip around the sun that was the catalyst for change, and I decided to celebrate differently. I didn't want a big party; I didn't want a big fuss . . . what I really wanted was solitude and time to remember who the hell I was!

So, I gifted myself a solo retreat to Bali!

I wasn't exactly sure what was calling me to Bali because I never had a desire to travel there before, but the pull was intense and I was curious to know, why?

That.Trip.Changed.Everything.

The Balinese are such radiant souls connected deeply to themselves and their culture. There is an incredible energy emanating from the island and you can't help but feel safely held. The retreat was entirely centred on receiving. From the food and spa treatments to the workshops, yoga classes and day trips, every aspect was a celebration of self.

I slept the best I had slept in a long time. My mind stopped racing. I was completely in the moment and my body and soul were honoured with the time they needed to heal. The solitude

I craved was satisfied; it was sacred, and it enriched my life in so many ways. However, I also learnt an important lesson in balance - connection is just as sacred.

I connected with the most heart-centred women on that trip. In my search for solitude, I underestimated how much my soul yearned for connection. We sat with cups of tea, relaxed in the sun, laughed and held space for one another, and I finally understood what was calling me to Bali. It wasn't just the solitude and connection; it was the opportunity to meet myself. The real self. The self that was free of the anger, resentment, grief, guilt and mental exhaustion that I had been carrying for far too long. This dedicated self-honouring time away, allowed me to return home a far better human than when I left and my perception of my life and my role in it changed irrevocably.

Loving and honouring yourself can come with a stigma. You might be thought of as selfish, conceited or vain. But who is looking after you, if you're not? Your entire wellbeing depends on it! You can't quite comprehend the enormity of self-neglect though, until you are so close to the end of your tether that all you can see is its frayed end.

There is a quote on the wall of my daughter's room that has been there since before she was born. It reads, 'Let her sleep. For when she wakes, she will move mountains'.

I know, without a shadow of doubt, that when you honour yourself and allow for rest, stillness and self-time with a healthy balance of connection, you come back fiercer than ever.

Self-Honouring Promise

My experience in Bali will forever be etched into my soul. If there is one thing I want to inspire in you, it's to intentionally carve out some time for yourself to reconnect, recalibrate and recentre. You don't necessarily need to go on an overseas trip (although I can't recommend it highly enough) but, at the very least, begin with a promise to honour what you need.

My Self-Honouring Promise

When I am feeling sad, I will . . .
When I worry about the future, I will . . .
When I am feeling stressed, I will . . .

When I feel uncomfortable in my body, I will remind myself of . . .
When I start comparing myself to other people, I will remind myself of . . .
When I find myself making excuses, I will remind myself of . . .

I choose to say no when . . .
I choose to celebrate when . . .
I choose to treat myself with . . .

ALIGNMENT AFFIRMATION

I am healthy. I am strong. I am healing.

CHAPTER NINETEEN

Roarsome

Being creative gets me high.

I am in flow and at my absolute best when I am in creation mode.

I actually thought I was clever and created a whole new word . . . but not according to Google. Roarsome already exists! It's a playful way of expressing that something is beyond awesome, in other words, exceptional.

Creativity is the lifeblood of the extraordinary. Being roarsome means breaking free from conventions and forging new paths. It's about daring to be different. However, it's common to be discouraged when witnessing others' innovation and entrepreneurship and you might begin to doubt your ability to bring something unique into the world. In my coaching, I often hear people express concerns like "I lack creativity" or "I can't create something entirely original that hasn't already been thought into existence". In reality, creativity resides within everyone; it's simply a matter of uncovering your personal X-factor.

Possessing the X-factor is what distinguishes you from the rest. Consider the iconic Beatles, whose groundbreaking music transformed the industry. Similarly, Pink's bold and authentic lyrics fearlessly tackle taboo subjects, demonstrating how embracing your individuality can inspire and resonate with others. Crossing art forms there's the prolific Stephen King whose stories are not only best sellers in their own right but have spawned a host of hugely successful films. And let's not forget George Lucas, the visionary behind Star Wars, whose X-factor birthed an entire universe that continues to captivate audiences. These icons serve as a reminder that the pursuit of the exceptional is a gamble worth taking, for it's in the uncharted territories of creativity that the X-factor truly flourishes.

It's important to acknowledge that creativity isn't just limited to traditional arts like painting or music; it extends to problem-solving, innovation, and everyday choices. Accepting your unique brand of creativity is a pivotal step towards personal growth and fulfillment. Each individual possesses a distinct creative fingerprint, shaped by their experiences, perspectives, and passions. Uncovering and embracing your creativity, allows you to uncover hidden talents and express yourself authentically.

To be creative and roarsome is to defy expectations, to explore the uncharted territory of your imagination. It's a journey filled with risk and reward but remember that the world craves diversity. By recognizing and celebrating your individual creativity, you contribute to a richer, more vibrant tapestry of human expression (more on this in Part 3). So, accept that your creativity is distinctive and unique, and recognise its power to elevate you daily to beyond awesome into exceptional.

What's your X-factor?

What is your X-factor and how can you apply it to a creative pursuit?

ALIGNMENT AFFIRMATION

I am open to creative possibilities.

CHAPTER TWENTY

Curiosity Did Not Kill the Cat

I love to learn.

Some would call me a perpetual learner. My heart and mind are always open to new ways of looking at the world and my place in it.

From four years of age, I always wanted to be a fashion designer.

When I was in preschool, paper bags were still used for groceries (funny how this has come back around now with the push towards a plastic free society!). I remember during one particular craft activity; I had free reign of the craft table to create anything I wanted. I grabbed a paper bag and cut down the middle of it. I then cut a round hole at the top for my head and arm holes at the sides and made myself a vest. I finished it off by decorating it with colourful patty pans. My teacher was so impressed with what I had created on my own that she sent me to the 'Blue Room' which was the BIG KIDS' room to show them what I had made - it was a big deal for a four-year-old. This was the beginning of my love affair with fashion and design. I spent the next twelve years designing and creating, with a particular interest in theatre costume. I studied Textiles and Design for four years in high school, I modelled in fashion parades, and I gained work experience at a very prestigious fashion school - I had finally found my way into making my dream a reality.

It was also my undoing!

In my stint of work experience, I endured a week immersed in an atmosphere saturated with pretentiousness and copious amounts of photocopying. As a high school kid trying to navigate my way through this industry, I faced numerous disdainful glances and audible sighs of frustration, with no one instilling any confidence in myself or the fashion industry. The environment exuded a cutthroat vibe, and I swiftly realised that my creativity and soul would not be nourished there. I returned home on my final day decisively abandoning my dream of becoming a fashion designer.

The second week of my work experience was at the Children's Hospital. These five short days piqued my curiosity for something I had never really even considered, and it ended up completely changing the course of my life. Each moment at the hospital was both at the same time confronting and inspirational. To be able to observe all the incredible things being done for these very ill children, from technological advancements, to fundraising, to housing for families so they could be close to their child while they received treatments; I got to experience it all. It filled me with so much hope. The hospital even ran a school for kids that were well enough to attend while they were there. This opened my eyes and heart to the possibility of being a teacher.

After graduating high school, I spent the next four years at university studying for a bachelor's degree in Primary Education. I then went on to teach for five years before stopping to concentrate on raising a family. But it wasn't long before my heart and mind went in search of more learning. While I was pregnant with my first son, I became curious about how aromatherapy could help during pregnancy and labour, so I completed a Diploma in Aromatherapy. While I was pregnant with my second son, I learnt how to be a 'Kinda Dance' teacher, traveling to preschools to teach dance and movement classes, which appealed to my creative dance and drama side. And while I was pregnant with my daughter my curiosity and passion for travel came to the fore and I completed a Diploma in Travel and Tourism.

I remember my dad saying to me once, "Len, pick one thing and stick with it".

But I have come to accept that sticking with only one thing just isn't who I am. The more I learnt, the more doors opened for me. Though unbeknownst to me, the biggest learning was still to come.

In 2015, after my dad died, I felt like everything I had learnt and worked towards no longer held any meaning. The reality of life's fragility hit me, and I questioned EVERYTHING. I sought to understand why my dad's heart and brain ceased to function, delving into the impact of stress on wellbeing. I pondered how life could still hold meaning after such a profound loss and I yearned to grasp the essence of truly living, not merely existing. There was an abundance of knowledge I longed to acquire.

It was this curiosity and sense of purpose that led me to study Holistic Counselling. I wanted to help people take ownership of their life without fear. Eight years later, I still love what I do, and I do it with passion in my heart and a fire in my belly. But it took a long time to get here. I realised I hadn't always been driven by passion, but I was always driven by curiosity and my most profound learning has been that, when you keep following your curiosity, it may in fact lead you to where your passion lies. Once you have found your passion you have what you need to align your life with all you intend it to be.

Get Curious

1. List all the things you have been curious about learning or places you have wanted to visit.
2. Circle your top three curiosities and make a plan to learn more about them.

ALIGNMENT AFFIRMATION

Nurturing my curiosity opens me up to new possibilities and creative solutions.

CHAPTER TWENTY-ONE

Pawsative Energy

I am not always a positive person.

Far from it some days.

Sometimes, there is no amount of yoga, meditation or positive affirmations that can lift the burden of the world from my shoulders. When this happens, I know it's because I am out of alignment with what I know is true and right and it is hugely impacted by the energy that has been circulating within my immediate environment.

I am highly empathic. Which simply means I have the ability to understand and share the feelings of others, perhaps more so than others. It is both a superpower and a curse. It is essential in my line of work as a transformative coach, but I can also be physically, emotionally or mentally affected by a subtle change in another person's energy. I can pick it a mile away. I can walk into a room full of people and be knocked off my feet by the swirling mix of positive and negative energy. I can forget about going shopping at Christmas time. I pick up on the collective angst of shoppers within five minutes which then shows up in my body as nausea and head-spins.

Science tells us that everything is energy. Including ourselves. If you stripped our bodies right back to the core, what is there? Energy. So, it stands to reason that being surrounded by the energetic fields of other people will have an effect on your own energy and, depending on the nature of that energy, the effect can be one of expansion or contraction.

Expansion is positive and promotes growth and vitality while contraction is negative and leads to shutting down and closing off. If you are going to all the effort to align your life with your values, your intentions and the right people then you sure as hell need to make sure that you are aligning with the right energy, because that shit will send your lion tail into a spin.

How does one do this? So glad you asked!

Oprah Winfrey is quoted as saying that we are all personally responsible for the energy we bring into any room that we enter. A change in energy that is expansive needs to begin with you. If my energy is low and negative, you can bet your bottom dollar that it will affect everyone else in my household. If I consciously work on shifting my energy to one of expansion, then I witness this beautiful flow on effect with everyone around me. I achieve this shift in a number of ways:

- Steering clear of social media, the news and radio - it's rarely good news so don't put yourself through that hell.
- Getting out into nature - negative ions are abundant in nature and believed to increase the mood hormone serotonin which helps to alleviate symptoms of depression, stress and anxiety.

- Exercising - Yin Yoga is more my speed which is a more meditative yoga practice and allows for internal expansion through contemplation.
- Meditating - yes, I will keep plugging the benefits of meditation until the day I die. Do a little experiment - observe the energy of a person who meditates compared to a person who doesn't. What do you notice?
- Withdrawing from social situations - saying no to people or events that are not conducive to expansion is not selfish, it's self-protection. A big part of self-acceptance is also accepting when certain situations or groups of people are not aligned with who you are. Give of your time and energy in small doses.
- Self-Educating - I absolutely love investing in hearing someone inspiring speak live. I have been in the presence of His Holiness the Dalia Lama, Gabrielle Bernstein, Deepak Chopra, Elizabeth Gilbert, Sarah Jessica Parker and Marianne Williamson. Each person gifted me a different way to look at the world and my place in it. New knowledge is, in itself, expanding!
- Listening to music - streaming or live, either way, music has the ability to shift your energy.
- Solitude - alone time whether at home or away somewhere blissful, it is crucial for replenishing your energy, especially when you have been around a lot of different people for an extended period of time.

Create A Plan for Expansion

1. Draw up two columns. Label one *What Expands Me?* and label the other one *What Contracts Me?* Fill in the table with all the people, places, hobbies, activities etc

that expand or contract you. Spend more time in the expansion column!
2. Make a list of people who inspire you and seek opportunities to learn from them or hear them speak.
3. Create your own high-vibe playlist to listen to in those times of contraction.

ALIGNMENT AFFIRMATION

I expand by letting go of all that no longer serves me.

CHAPTER TWENTY-TWO

Prepare for the Uproar

I've lost friends.

It happens and it's crappy. But not as crappy as having to hide who you really are for fear of outshining someone else.

My friend, the time has come to step into those big, padded paws and prepare yourself for the part of your personal transformation that is a culmination of all your deep inner work. It is also the most challenging part because it generally comes with a bit of an uproar.

If there is something I am certain about it's that not everyone you know will get onboard with your radical transformation. Your determination to make changes will scare people. Your vulnerability will be met with discomfort. People will laugh, ridicule, and condemn you before they even consider that you are evolving into this beautiful outward expression of who you truly are.

Similar to many other people, I've struggled with tying my self-worth and success to the number of *likes* and *followers* on social media. Experiencing the shame of someone unfriending or unfollowing my page because expressing my vulnerabilities, celebrating my successes or sharing my knowledge was a bridge too far, has often led me to consider returning to my 'cage'. Social media should never serve as the yardstick for one's value and worth.

You are preparing yourself for my favourite part of the transformative process and that is self-expression - where you really get to embody who you are.

If you have ever observed a small child, you see them show up as a true expression of themselves, no inhibitions, no cares about what people think, just carefree and wild. That is because they have not yet learned to hide who they are from the world. They have not learned to mould themselves into what society deems 'acceptable'.

The act of breaking through the mould you have been cast in by those around you and journeying back to the core of who you are will be met by three types of uproarious animals: lions and tigers and bears!

Lions will companion with you. These are the people who support your growth, your need for change and individualism. They will encourage and challenge you while, at the same time, holding you to your highest potential.

Tigers will be vicious in their attacks on you. These are the people who watch and wait and then pounce if you step out of line, trying to convince you that you are not who you believe yourself to be.

Bears will smother you. These are the people who will try to hug you to death, holding you so close for fear of losing you and who you used to be. These are usually the friends who fall away because they don't understand your journey.

The uproar doesn't just come from other people either, it will also come from yourself. Every doubt, pain and trauma will be there to greet you at every bend and turn in your journey to attempt to make you forget who the hell you are and what you're made of. All your inner demons will resurface to remind you that you're not as great as you think you are.

I'm not selling this whole transformation thing, am I? Why would you bother?

Because in the midst of the external and internal conflict, when you are frustrated, angry or lonely and when the same old way of living, responding and thriving aren't working for you anymore, you realise the power lies entirely within you and you have a choice to do things differently.

The uproar actually supports your journey in more ways than is first evident. By being challenged, attacked and smothered it catalyses the need to step into a complete and beautiful expression of who you are and how you want to show up in the world.

For me:

> The lions taught me to trust myself.
> The tigers taught me to fight for myself.
> The bears taught me to let go.

You need to learn to be okay with an uproar. It's an inevitable part of any transformation. Some people will be left behind, some people will never understand you, some will continue to laugh, ridicule and condemn but your ability to push past them is the greatest acknowledgement of self-acceptance and the moment the true expression of who you are is revealed.

Declaration

Make a declaration of what you are accepting about yourself whole-heartedly and that which you will never be apologetic for.

How will you trust yourself?
How will you fight for yourself?
What will you let go of?

ALIGNMENT AFFIRMATION

With love and grace, I step forward with courage.

PART THREE

SELF-EXPRESSION

Be Yourself

How will you show up in the world as a true expression of yourself?

You now have awareness of who you are and have accepted this enough to make changes in your life where you weren't in alignment with who you want to be. But you can't show up as your true authentic self if you can't express it yourself to those around you. If you feel afraid to live as a beautiful expression of who you are then you are still hiding. It took me a long time to learn this and be okay with it. I know now that when I connect with people and I am able to have deep and meaningful conversations with them, if they are interested in what I have to say then I know those people genuinely want to be a part of my life because they are connecting with the real me . . . not a semi-hidden version of me. At the end of each of the following chapters, you are encouraged to take courageous (and sometimes rebellious) action to step into the truest expression of yourself and share it with the world unapologetically.

CHAPTER TWENTY-THREE

IT'S A JUNGLE OUT THERE

Sometimes I am afraid of the world we live in.

In many ways, it's a world that still prevents individuals from authentically expressing themselves. It instils fear in me as I contemplate how I will equip my children to not only navigate it but flourish as their true selves. There is this lingering concern that they might end up living as mere echoes of who they could be, mirroring the reality of so many people in the world today.

Then I remember that it starts with me. I am the one who needs to show up as a full expression of myself. I need to show my children that with enough courage, strength and understanding of themselves that they know it is safe to do the same and live their life as the person they were meant to be.

I wrote a letter to my daughter when she was six, on International Women's Day 2020, in the hopes that one day it may help her navigate the jungle she may find herself in. But really, its message is not just for her. It's for you too. My hope is that it may help you remember who you are meant to be so that you can make your own way through the jungle out there - undiminished and living as your authentic self.

I knew motherhood was going to come with some big challenges. I knew I wasn't going to get it right all the time. I knew I would make mistakes, and we would yell and scream at each other. I knew I would make decisions that were right for me but not necessarily right for you. But my biggest challenge as a mum has been to stop proving to people that you are worthy of their love and attention.

Over the last six years, one of the greatest gifts I have had is time. Time to sit back and watch how things have played out; how people interact with you, how people speak to you, how people give of their time for you and how people unintentionally disempower you.

I have also had time to watch you thrive, to develop a sense of who you are, to stand your ground when you feel strongly enough about something and to voice your concerns about the world and the people in it.

As your mum, I spend so much time trying to control your behaviour because I worry about what other people will think. I now realise what a mistake that is, because all it does is give them the power to control who you are. Until you're a mum, it is hard to comprehend how one little person can both fill your heart and break it at the same time, but it happens—daily.

You see, I want so much for you. I want you to feel loved and supported and protected. I want you to feel like you matter, but the problem is I want other people to do the same for you and some won't. So, it is important to me that you know that you don't need to look for that outside of yourself.

On International Women's Day 2020, here is what I know and what I want you to know:

When people don't respond to you the way you expect them to, it's because they don't know how to respond to someone they can't control.

When you are told that you are too loud, it's because they don't know how to respond to someone who knows how to use their voice.

When comments are made about the 'petiteness' of other girls your age right in front of you, it's because those people use weight as a standard of measurement for worthiness. It should never be a measurement of your worth . . . ever.

When you are told you are strong-willed in such a way that it is something to be ashamed of, my darling, you dig your heels in even more. Show them how strong-willed you can be, because you are showing them what they themselves are afraid to do.

I am not interested in whether you are the best reader in class, or whether you have the most friends or if you can do cartwheels, back flips or tumble turns better than others or whether you are somebody's 'favourite'. The only thing I am interested in is that you are raised to be a decent human being, one that goes through life helping others to rise.

I have had the gift of time.

Time to get to know you better than you know yourself right now.

But that won't always be the case.

The way I know you is never going to get you to where you want to be in life. To get where you want to go, there will come a time when you will need to know yourself better than anyone. This begins with giving yourself permission to be who you want to be regardless of other people's love and attention.

Use that strong will to change the world. You come from a line of strong women who have your back no matter what and with that you can do anything.

How are you going to show up in the world? What will it take to untangle yourself from the clawing tendrils and vines of the jungle's undergrowth so that you can live life unapologetically as yourself?

REBELLIOUS ACTION

Notice who you spend time with. Do these people allow you to live as who you are meant to be? Find one person you resonate with and intentionally carve out some extra time with them.

CHAPTER TWENTY-FOUR

Hear Me Roar

I have a strong sense of justice.

But I have had to work on improving how I express it.

Within you resides an inner truth yearning for expression. The pursuit of this truth has the ability to nurture genuine connections, personal growth, and emotional wellbeing. On the other hand, there can be a hidden cost of concealing your thoughts and emotions instead of openly expressing them.

There have been numerous occasions where conversations have left me feeling disempowered, shamed or ridiculed. There were certainly moments when I strongly desired to make it unmistakably clear that I was extremely pissed-off by something someone had said. However, I grappled with the dilemma of choosing between maintaining harmony by staying silent or risk being perceived as difficult, unreasonable or overly reactive if I spoke my mind. All too often, I chose the path of silence, bearing the weight of unspoken words, which manifested as tremendous emotional and physical upheaval. My body reacted with a persistent tight throat and chest, a racing heart, and intense anger. But, as I came to discover, the effort required to suppress my words and emotions proved to be far more taxing than the reality of openly expressing them.

Speaking out against injustice can be incredibly daunting. There are moments when you're aware that something is not right, yet the fear of being shunned silences you like a gag of gaffer tape. As you begin to work through layers of growth you will begin to discover that you have a very clear message that demands expression. It is important to notice in which situations you may be restraining yourself unnecessarily and seek opportunities to speak truthfully with love and kindness.

When you begin to express your authentic thoughts, feelings, and beliefs, you not only honour your own identity but foster opportunities for profound connections with others. It's important to nurture and express your own authentic voice. When you don't, external influences can overpower your sense of self, leading to self-doubt and confusion about your values and path in life. Embracing and using your own voice helps you stay true to yourself and your convictions. It lays the foundation for open and honest communication, allowing you to address misunderstandings, resolve conflicts and, as a result, cultivate deep trust in relationships. By acknowledging your emotions and experiences, you pave the way for personal growth and a deeper understanding and appreciation of yourself.

When a lion roars, it resonates across distances of up to 5 miles away (approx. 8km). Now, consider the profound influence your voice can have if you wholeheartedly embrace it. Speaking your truth stands as a powerful expression of self-awareness and self-acceptance. As you grow more at ease with this, you pave the way for others to do the same. Ultimately, this liberates you from the burden of unspoken words and enables your soul to flourish in the most authentic and unrestricted way possible.

REBELLIOUS ACTION

For the sake of what are you willing to speak your truth, even if your voice shakes? Practice speaking it out loud. When the moment presents itself, speak it for real.

CHAPTER TWENTY-FIVE

YOUR HIGHEST PURR-TENTIAL

I haven't reached my highest potential.

Yet.

Bruce Lee famously said, *"Always be yourself, express yourself, have faith in yourself, do not go out and look for a successful personality, and duplicate it."*

I find inspiration in those actively pursuing dreams I only envision. Yet, at times, I've doubted the possibility that I have the potential to attain similar dreams. I have felt like an imposter, I have second-guessed my skills, and I have very much thought that I know less than I actually do. As a result, this has prevented me from expressing my wants, needs and truths for many years. I was afraid, not of who I am, but who I might become and whether I was worthy.

Prior to my journey to Bali, I had a sense that I was on the correct path with my coaching practice, yet I grappled with this uncomfortable feeling that something was amiss. It wasn't until

I found solitude in a foreign country, far away from the familiar, that I realised what was right in front of me all along. I had consistently been trying to portray a version of myself that wasn't genuine. I was trying to find myself in other people and not realising that I actually get to create myself exactly as I want. This showed up in how I expressed myself to other people about what I do and why I do it.

Poet, Mark Nepo, points out that the people we tend to admire through life, the ones we try to emulate, are like the moon - they just reflect back to us what is already there. You don't need to copy or envy others; you need to uncover what is within yourself.

Unlocking your highest potential is a journey through self-awareness, self-acceptance, self-expression and relentless determination. It involves pushing boundaries, embracing challenges, and continuously learning from both successes and setbacks. There is no recipe, formula or script for achieving this. It's complex, highly personal and damn hard work!

However, a growth mindset is essential. Surround yourself with a supportive environment and seek knowledge and guidance from a wide range of sources and people - not to become a clone but to gather fuel for your own fire. You will never reach YOUR highest potential if you are pretending to be someone else. It's okay to be inspired and learn from successful people but don't be an expression of them. Being someone else requires more effort and poses more challenges than distilling what you have learnt and allowing what is naturally yours to shine through.

Reaching your highest potential is not about achieving goals, these are the pleasant by-products of your journey, but it's also about evolving into the best version of yourself, realising qualities and capabilities you might not have known existed. It's an ongoing process of self-improvement, fuelled by an unwavering belief in your capacity to roar to new heights as a true expression of yourself.

REBELLIOUS ACTION

What is one thing you need to do in order to reach your highest potential? What is the very next thing you need to do to put it into action?

CHAPTER TWENTY-SIX

ONE IN A MIL-LION

Competition doesn't worry me.

I know how to 'stay in my own lane'.

In my household, we frequently employ this phrase. When someone begins to doubt their capabilities, becomes preoccupied with others' actions, succumbs to comparison, or feels entangled in constant competition, I rely on this valuable reminder. If you divert your attention for even a second to gauge others' progress in their journey, you risk losing sight of your ultimate goal. This may cause you to slow down or even abandon your pursuits. My son and husband each have a post-it note on their desk bearing the message "Stay in your own lane" as a reminder not to aspire to be anything other than their authentic selves.

"The coaching industry is flooded".

If I received a dollar for every instance, I've heard this, I'd be financially set for life. However, had I embraced this notion each time it was mentioned, my business wouldn't have thrived. I wouldn't have written this book, nor would I have reached and helped as many individuals confidently and proudly hold themselves to their highest potential.

Within my industry, some have remarked that my offerings are indistinguishable from countless other coaches, given the prevalence of coaches empowering women. To this, I acknowledge that while that observation might hold some truth, none of those coaches are me. I don't see the coaching landscape with undue optimism, nor do I believe everyone will seek my services or that I can assist everyone I encounter. What I do recognise is that no one on this planet is exactly like me and my unique style, message and personality will resonate with the individuals who truly need it.

What I need from you my friend, is to approach life with the same conviction.

I want you to stop looking around you to see what other people are doing and stay in your own lane. I want you to hold firmly who you are and what your uniqueness brings to the world. I want you to fully embrace the true expression of who you are, and I want you to never back down in the face of others pursuing similar paths because you are one in a mil-lion . . . actually you are once in a lifetime and this life time is way too bloody short to be worrying about measuring up to everybody else.

REBELLIOUS ACTION

What is your point of difference? What makes you a one in a million kind of person? Find it and express it with confidence!

CHAPTER TWENTY-SEVEN

THE LION'S DEN

I am easily turned on.

By a man who knows how to empower a woman.

Recently, a significant movement toward gender equality has emerged, and it is well-deserved. Progress is being achieved, but there is still more ground to cover. The timeless question of what women really want, is finally being addressed. We are becoming more vocal, advocating for the right to be acknowledged and heard. Nevertheless, in our quest for visibility, I feel we may have unintentionally disempowered our male counterparts. I have worked with men in my coaching who confess they are fearful of voicing their own needs due to potential backlash.

I had an epiphany regarding this when I found myself in a conversation with my husband one evening, expressing my frustration about the fact that he had his own retreat, his *Man Cave* (aka our garage). In this sanctuary, he painted, played his guitar, and enjoyed his 80s rock band DVDs undisturbed. I was venting about my lack of such a space, to which he playfully retorted, "Well, you do have a space - it's the kitchen."

To be clear, he has never used that line on me again!

As I brooded in my own frustrations, I began to ponder why I should resent him having a retreat to escape all the *noise* of the world, a place for self-reflection, relaxation, and mental preparation for his various roles in life - husband, father, son, brother, teacher and friend. It had become clear that I had developed a sense of entitlement. I saw myself as his equal, deserving of such a space for myself. I questioned where I could find my own escape, where I could recharge. What I initially failed to understand was that in allowing him this refuge, I was actually recharging my most powerful ally, my unwavering support, my champion.

On my path to personal greatness, this man has watched me fall again and again. He has sat with me on the bathroom floor as my grief shattered me into pieces. He has cradled me through the heartache of two miscarriages and he has listened with empathy as I have expressed my desire to run from all the big feelings I didn't want to face. Yet, through it all, he remains by my side, expressing his pride in my accomplishments and unwavering belief in my efforts to help others.

Could I extend the same grace to him for expressing himself in those circumstances? I actually don't know. In some way, I've come to believe that I have the right to make these demands of him, without recognising that he also requires some of that in return.

The truth is, we aren't completely equal. Women weren't designed to perform every task a man can. Instead, women excel in areas where men may not, and vice versa. Frankly, it's a refreshing relief. I have no desire to shoulder all the responsibility and there are many things I'm genuinely thankful not to have on my plate.

For the past decade, I've dedicated myself to studying and exploring self-empowerment. I've surrounded myself with like-minded women to absorb their vibrant energy, invested in conferences and courses led by some of the most influential voices in our world today. However, the most profound source of empowerment has been within my very own home. My husband has my back, filling in where I fall short and handling what I can't. With a person like that in your life, whoever they may be, there's no need to juggle everything all the time. You uplift each other and focus on what you can do at different moments.

Do I *need* him in order to feel empowered within myself? No, I don't. I have made significant strides in empowering myself. Do I *want* him in my corner, cheering me on? Absolutely. Has his unwavering belief in me enhanced my life? Without a doubt.

We need to consider giving our male counterparts some room to regroup and recharge. They too have a right to express themselves. Let them find their own sanctuary, whether it's a man cave, a fishing trip, a golf game, a football field, or anything else, so that they can reemerge in a way that will further our pursuit of equality and acknowledgment. Hold them in the same esteem with which we now hold ourselves and remember to champion them into greatness also.

REBELLIOUS ACTION

Is there a man in your life that needs to be championed? (Note: this does not need to be a partner, it can be a father, father figure, brother, colleague etc). Make the time to let them know how valued they are.

CHAPTER TWENTY-EIGHT

Dande-lion

Discomfort is my superpower.

Even so, this doesn't mean I don't want to puke at the thought of pushing myself beyond my comfort zone!

Psychiatrist and author, M. Scott Peck says that our finest moments are most likely to occur when we are feeling deeply uncomfortable, unhappy or unfulfilled. For it is only in such moments, propelled by our discomfort, that we are motivated to step out of our ruts and start searching for different ways or truer answers.

I couldn't agree more.

Discomfort is where creativity thrives and signals a readiness for transformation. Throughout the history of human endeavour, our greatest achievements, discoveries and creations have all been propelled by a problem needing to be solved. Embracing discomfort paves the way for the extraordinary. Discomfort is the fuel that enables individuals to unlock untapped potential and foster expansion across all facets of life.

A dandelion is a wonderful example of expansion. It has a remarkable ability to spread and proliferate. Often seen as a nuisance weed, their fluffy seeds are carried by the wind, covering vast distances and taking root in all kinds of environments. They exemplify resilience and adaptability as they thrive in all sorts of uncomfortable conditions as they expand their presence.

Quite often, as individuals, we don't want to be seen as a nuisance taking up space and so we play small and stay safe in the confines of our comfort zone rather than learning to adapt, grow and flourish. We need to be like the dandelion. It doesn't care where it ends up, who it offends or the environment with which it has to contend. Instead, it always acts as a true expression of itself and in doing so, ultimately enables it to expand, grow and proliferate.

In between teaching, my husband did a stint in real estate. Something he learnt during that time that he often throws my way when I am being self-critical about my work is, "No one buys a secret". Meaning that unless you put yourself out there and expand beyond your comfort zone, no one will know you exist!

One of the most effective ways to expand is through self-expression. Articulating your thoughts, emotions and ideas leads to growth. When you express yourself, you build upon the foundation of self-awareness and self-acceptance that you have already laid. In doing so you are able to leverage this knowledge of who you are and what you want to become and fully realise your goals. Self-expression fosters empathy for, connection with and a deeper understanding and appreciation of other people. In return, they see the unfiltered version of you. As you expand and connect, you are introduced to diverse viewpoints, often challenging your own beliefs, but always broadening your worldview. The act of self-expression, whether through words, art or even how you dress, has the ability to propel you far beyond your comfort zone, perhaps even farther than you imagined, facilitating a broad expansion in both self-perception and your relationships with others.

Once you surrender to expansion in all its forms, your growth allows you to become more self-aware of issues that keep arising for you and helps prepare you to address them. You begin to let go of past hurts, develop a deeper understanding of your thoughts and feelings, start to speak up about things you feel strongly about but most importantly, despite the fear and uncertainty that keeps you bound and gagged within the confines of your comfort zone, you become limitless in the pursuit of reclaiming your authentic self.

REBELLIOUS ACTION

Commit to doing something that expands you beyond your comfort zone.

CHAPTER TWENTY-NINE

LEAVING YOUR PAW PRINT

I care about what others think of me.

To a certain extent.

I'm not bothered with people's opinions about my clothing, hairstyle, gym attendance, beliefs or profession. Nevertheless, I am deeply invested in the impact I have on others and the lasting impression I create.

I have pondered this a lot over the years, particularly in the aftermath of my dad's passing. He was a respected pharmacist in the community, who offered guidance, support, and immense kindness to all he encountered, far more than I could ever match. However, following his passing and the necessity to sell his pharmacy, the term "legacy" was frequently discussed.

Many people believed his pharmacy represented his legacy, and there was a strong sentiment that one of his children should assume control of the business.

I found myself being mildly amused by this. Aside from the significant detail that none of his children were licensed pharmacists, which is rather crucial, it surprised me that people believed his legacy to be his pharmacy. That four walls with medication, various body products and a cash register was who my dad was. He was so much more.

How he raised his children, his guidance, the comfort he provided when our lives seemed to crumble and the support he offered in pursuing our own unique paths, rather than pharmacy, that was his true legacy. I carry these teachings with me daily, and, more importantly, I can pass them onto my children.

It wasn't what he did for a living, it was who he was as a person and that, my friend, is what I want you to take from this. Look at what you are doing right now. Who are you? How do you show up for yourself and others? How do you make people feel in your presence? This is your legacy.

My inner circle consists of a handful of select and very special people. These are the people whose opinion really matters to me. The most important of these are my children. The ones who benefit the most from the 'paw prints' I leave behind. A legacy is an expression of who you are. It is a gift that can be handed down. My dad handed down wisdom, courage, insight, strength, faith and a cheeky sense of humour so I could hand these down to my children.

Buddhist monk Thich Nhat Hanh said, 'The only thing that remains after you die are the consequences of your actions of body, speech and mind'. A legacy doesn't need to be a grand gesture. You don't need to invest anything, start anything, donate anything (although you can if you want) but sometimes your legacy can be as simple as showing others how best to live that will resonate beyond your lifetime.

REBELLIOUS ACTION

How do you want to be remembered? Write a kick-ass, one sentence epitaph!

CHAPTER THIRTY

The Cowardly Lion

I don't always want to be brave.

Sometimes I want other people to be brave for me.

With a title like *The Cowardly Lion*, one might expect this chapter to be about bravery and courage. Initially it was.

But I changed my mind.

The day I penned this chapter, I was having a moment. As my children prepared themselves for school I gazed at my reflection in the bathroom mirror, and the person staring back at me tilted her head to one side, tears welling in her eyes and she said, "I can't do this anymore". She was overwhelmed, exhausted and defeated.

I've been quite open about my tendency to strive for progress. When confronted with a problem, I don't simply ignore it and hope it goes away; I scrutinise it from all angles and relentlessly seek solutions, occasionally pushing myself to the brink of mental and physical exhaustion, which is where I found myself staring into my bathroom mirror.

It didn't feel right for me to write a chapter centred on advocating bravery and courage, which sounds odd considering that the motivation for writing this book is to empower you to embody bravery and courage in your life and confront your fears. However, if I am to lead by example in being a full expression of myself and speak the truth then I felt that this chapter needed to express that it's okay to not be brave and courageous all the time. Ironically, it requires a certain level of bravery and courage to not be.

It takes a tremendous amount of bravery to ask for help. You can invest substantial effort in self-improvement, cultivating self-acceptance and expressing yourself authentically and unapologetically BUT that does not guarantee immunity from life's challenges. While these practices can certainly make life more manageable, they don't exempt you from experiencing moments of sadness, grief and frustration when people piss you off. It also doesn't mean that you need to maintain a relentlessly positive outlook in every situation. Adopting a mindset of soldiering on through life when you feel overwhelmed, isolated and exhausted is toxic and counterproductive to everything I have spoken about thus far.

What I need you to understand is that you don't always have to have your shit sorted out to undergo personal growth and transformation. A genuine display of bravery and courage occurs when you can assert with confidence and without shame "Today, I don't feel like being brave, I need someone else to step up and be brave for me". It's about gracefully stepping aside and allowing someone else to take the lead for a while.

REBELLIOUS ACTION

What is something you need help with and are too afraid to ask for it? Speak it out loud, then go find someone who can help.

CHAPTER THIRTY-ONE

RADICAL REBEL-LION

I am in love with a woman.

And I have completely hated her too.

I have raised her on a pedestal and told her how incredibly brave she is. I have also torn her to shreds and told her how worthless she is.

She is unapologetically herself and yet she still hides the true essence of who she is.

I have cradled her broken heart in my hands not knowing how to fix it. I have also helped her put it back together one piece at a time.

She wants other people to change the world with her, but she has also bravely taken steps to change the world on her own.

I have witnessed her lowest moments.

I have also marvelled at her greatest moments.

She has prevented herself from greatness for fear of what others may say but she has also stood in her greatness despite what others may say.

I have been pained by her need to control everything in her life. I have also felt her surrender to her life.

She has given her power away and suffered but she has also stood in her power and reaped the rewards.

I have gone to great lengths to silence her on numerous occasions. I have also stood back and let her speak her truth.

She has allowed other people to unfairly mistreat her but she has gone into fierce battle for those same people, so they knew they were loved.

I have watched her from the sidelines try to pretzel herself to fit into the image others hold of her, but I have also stood in awe of how she seems to find the courage to step outside that image and hold her own.

She has been paralysed by fear and yet looked fear in the eye and told it to back off.

I have looked on as she's screwed up again and again as a friend, mother, daughter and wife.

I have also watched her hold herself accountable for her actions.

She can be gracefully grounded and yet extremely anxious.

I have watched her safeguard her vulnerability.

But seen her turn it into her superpower.

She has climbed mountains only to fall down the other side. She has risen right in front of me.

I have lied to her incessantly.

But I have also spoken truth to her.

She is beautifully fragile but relentlessly fierce.

She curses and screams but laughs and sings.

She has been stopped but is unstoppable.

She overreacts but is level-headed.

She is loved by many and not liked by some.

She cares too much and doesn't care enough.

She is right and wrong.

She is lightness and darkness.
She is perfectly imperfect.
She is a rebel soul.
She is me.
Don't resolve to be one or the other.
Be all the things.

There is no shame in being a paradox, that's where your radical rebellion lies.

REBELLIOUS ACTION

Be a paradox!

CHAPTER THIRTY-TWO

Paws for Reflection

I'm not very good at staying still.

Unless I am forced to.

This chapter is brought to you by week eight of a Pandemic lockdown, when everyone was forced to be still!

I belong to that group of individuals who constantly crave activity. Without giving my mind something to occupy itself, it tends to run a mental marathon featuring my fears, failures and grievances. However, the lockdown period taught me to value moments of stillness. During these moments my self-awareness heightens. The neglected aspects of myself become more vocal, and the parts I've inadvertently ignored clamour for my attention. My usual rush from one task to another blinds me from reflecting on my past, my current state, and my future direction. I often overlook the progress I've made and the people who continue to support me.

Reflection can also grant you a moment of grace before immersing yourself in a situation with full intensity, providing a vital pause. If I hadn't taken the time to reflect and ponder my messaging before composing each of these chapters, this book would have taken a significantly different trajectory. Similarly, the pause I embraced to revisit and edit each chapter post-completion revealed to me in the most beautiful way that the person who embarked on writing this book is wildly different to the person who penned the final chapter. This transformation led me to reword many chapters, as personal growth had taught me to express myself in a new light. Without this evolution, the narrative would have been steered by anger and pain rather than wisdom and gratitude.

In this chapter, there are no major revelations, except the importance of embracing stillness. Self-reflection emerges as the silent hero behind any personal transformation. It's the moment when you can truly pause and assess the profoundly powerful journey you've embarked on.

REBELLIOUS ACTION

After reflecting, express yourself by celebrating wildly! Where have you been? What have you conquered? Who continues to support you? How will you celebrate this?

CHAPTER THIRTY-THREE

Reclaiming the Throne

I still don't have all my cubs in a row.

One of those little buggers always manages to step out of line! But I don't need all my cubs in a row to fiercely pursue more in life.

When I wholeheartedly committed to a career in transformative coaching, I hadn't confronted all my shadows before diving in to assist others with theirs. I aspired to be a rescuer, which might seem positive, but it has its drawbacks. While serving those genuinely in need is commendable, playing the perpetual rescuer inadvertently disempowers those you are helping and hinders their growth. Constantly taking on this role shifts the focus away from your own unresolved issues. Despite succeeding in helping others, you cannot neglect the need to address your own challenges and desires.

I think mastering your life as a whole is impossible. As it goes along, life continually offers new lessons and perspectives. Yet,

I do believe in mastering the three key areas covered in this book to enhance your human experience. Neglecting any of these areas will leave you feeling like a victim to life rather than a victor.

I can't guide you on how to be yourself. The work is yours alone to do. What I have offered you, through owning my own truths, quirks, losses and wins, is the framework for reclaiming what is naturally yours. You must take the next steps using the tools and concepts within the pages of this book if you so choose and trust that as you undertake your journey that more tools and meaningful connections will emerge to aid you as you go.

The Egyptian goddess Sekhmet, whose name signifies strength and might, commanded both power and dread. Frequently portrayed as a lioness or a woman with a lion's head, she embodies the captivating duality of light and dark within oneself. As the goddess of war and plague, she was fierce and temperamental, yet she also held the roles of healing and protection. Her complexity rendered her both feared and revered, a goddess of intricate nature.

Like Sekhmet, reclaiming your own power is about striking a balance between healer and warrior. It is a dance between self-awareness, self-acceptance and self-expression, to be able to heal the parts that need healing, accepting the parts that need accepting and expressing the parts that need expressing with unwavering self-belief. Embracing every facet of your inner self, be it positive or negative, light or dark, aggressive or gentle, driven or patient, emotional or stoic, masculine or feminine, is essential. To present yourself as the most powerful and whole version of who you are, denying none of these aspects is crucial.

In a standout moment from a beloved Marvel film, *Black Panther: Wakanda Forever*, Shuri, the sister of the late Black Panther, faces off against M'Baku, leader of the Jabari tribe, in a strength testing encounter to prove her worthiness as the new Black Panther. She stares him down with fierce determination while engaging in an arm wrestle, which she ultimately wins. This triumph not only cements her own unwavering self-belief but also signifies her reclaiming the mantle of Black Panther and by extension her rightful place on the throne.

Reclaiming your throne is not about finding your power, it's about remembering it's there and using it to not only elevate yourself but elevate others.

When you know yourself, own yourself and be yourself, you can stare life down with fierce determination and assert your place in the world and confidently reclaim the space that rightfully belongs to you. There is a rather precarious bridge that exists between fear and courage that you will need to step onto in order to truly embrace that 'Leo' personality and often you will need to step onto it before you feel ready, before you have all your cubs in a row. If you don't learn to master it, you run the risk of living your life on the dark side of fear and miss out on what the light side of courage has to offer you. When you possess this fierce self-belief, no one can shame you or make you feel less than you are and if they try then let me impart the best advice my dad ever gave me - if anyone hurts you, criticises you or ridicules you, live to prove them wrong.

To finish with the words I began with, there is no shame in desiring more from your life. There comes a time when holding onto the facade of who you pretend to be becomes much harder than standing strong in the truth of who you really are. Can you feel it? You are beginning to awaken. There is a fierce leonine energy that dwells in your soul. The world is yearning for people like you to show courage and step into your greatness.

Your time is now.

REBELLIOUS ACTION

Step into your greatness, with fierce determination.

The Tail End

List of self-awareness check-in questions

What traits are you hiding in the shadows? How can you look at these differently?

Where in your life are you not calling the shots? Decide to change that.

Where in your life are you being tamed? Who is doing the taming?

Are you the victim of crabs? When in your life have you been a crab?

What is getting in the way of you showing up for your child/ren?

How can you develop your relationships with children so that you become someone they want to spend time with?

What imperfections in life do you need to embrace?

What bullshit lies do you keep telling yourself?

Where is fear taking over your life? How are you projecting this fear onto others?

What thorns are you concealing? How can you deal with your anger assertively?

What failures of yours have become lessons?
What do you need to forgive yourself for?

List of alignment affirmations

I allow my inner guide to show me the way.
I am worthy of a healthy, supportive, loving relationship.
I am making room for amazing people to enter my life.
Every day I become clearer about the boundaries that serve me best.
I choose my own definition of what it means to be enough.
My intentions are honourable and serve the highest good.
I am healthy, I am strong, I am healing.
I am open to creative possibilities.
Nurturing my curiosity opens me up to new possibilities and creative solutions.
I expand by letting go of all that no longer serves me.
With love and grace, I step forward with courage.

List of rebellious actions

Notice who you spend time with. Do these people allow you to live as who you are meant to be? Find one person you resonate with and intentionally carve out some extra time with them.

For the sake of what are you willing to speak your truth, even if your voice shakes? Practice speaking it out loud. When the moment presents itself, speak it for real.

What is one thing you need to do in order to reach your highest potential? What is the very next thing you need to do to put it into action?

What is your point of difference? What makes you a one in a mil-lion kind of person? Find it and express it with confidence!

Is there a man in your life that needs to be championed? (Note: this does not need to be a partner, it can be a father, father figure, brother, colleague etc). Make the time to let them know how valued they are.

Commit to doing something that expands you beyond your comfort zone.

How do you want to be remembered? Write a kick-ass, one sentence epitaph!

What is something you need help with and are too afraid to ask for it? Speak it out loud, then go find someone who can help.

Be a paradox!

After reflecting, express yourself by celebrating wildly! Where have you been? What have you conquered? Who continues to support you? How will you celebrate this?

Step into your greatness, with fierce determination.

Other helpful resources

The Dark Side of the Light Chasers - Debbie Ford
How To Do the Work - Dr. Nicole LePera
The Language of Emotions - Karla McLaren
Everything is Figureoutable - Marie Forleo
The Seven Principles for Making Marriage Work - John Gottman
Wired For Love - Stan Tatkin

What contributed to my inner transformation?

Stillness and a healthy amount of solitude
Reading A LOT!
Learning A LOT!
Yoga
Meditation

Dancing
Finding meaningful work
Meaningful connections with others
Owning my shit and committing to being better than I was the day before.

ACKNOWLEDGEMENTS

I'm not sure if there is a standard format you are supposed to follow when you write your acknowledgements, but after reading this book, you would be aware that I don't really play by the rules! In my first book, I think I acknowledged everyone I knew, but this time I'm more intentional with my gratitude. So, at the top of my list are my husband and kids because they had to hear about this book the most and put up with my demands for cups of tea, shoulder rubs, editing and relentless bouts of imposter syndrome.

Stu, Toby, Lucas and Audrey - you four make me want to be a better version of myself every single day. Stu, I knew I married the best, but you continue to support and encourage me without question, even when I don't deserve it, you have some serious gumption my love. Kids, I know I screw up, repeatedly, but the grace you show me is . . . clearly something you don't get from me! I honestly have no words to describe the awe I experience when I am in your presence. Super proud mumma!

Thank you to my mum, sister and brother for finally taking my advice on a lot of things and not just thinking that I'm talking a whole lot of mumbo jumbo. It's been quite a journey for the four of us but we are all starting to find our centre of gravity again and for that I am truly proud. Go us!!

To my angel friend Delly. We haven't even met in person, and you are one of the very few people who make me feel seen and heard. You are one of those once in a lifetime people and I am so honoured you are one of my people. Thank you for always believing in me, my work and my writing and for always knowing the right things to say. Also thank you for being weird with me. We all need a friend we can be weird with.

Finally, you, my friend, reading this book. I deeply appreciate the time you've taken to read my thoughts. My hope is that the words within these pages guide you to confidently reveal yourself to the world. I eagerly anticipate witnessing you fiercely embrace your true self.

ABOUT THE AUTHOR

Lenore is a passionate transformative coach and trained yoga teacher, known for her expertise in personal growth and holistic healing. Her book, *Self Ashored,* earned her the international BIBA Award for Best Self-Help in 2020 and the Cadmus Book Award in 2023. In 2021, she was honoured as Wellness Peacemaker of the Year for her impactful work in holistic counselling and transformative coaching in the field of Dispute Resolution.

Lenore's coaching style mirrors her approach to life - full of sass, introspection, and a whole lot of kick-ass energy. With a cheeky sense of humour, she masterfully blends deep life lessons with a safe space where people feel truly seen, heard, and supported on their journey to self-discovery. When she's not supporting others, you'll find her sipping tea, practicing yoga, meditating or escaping to some blissful retreat.

- Website - www.lenorepearson.com
- Email - lenorepearsonholistic@gmail.com
- Facebook - Lenore Pearson - Transformative Coaching
- Instagram - lenorepearson_holistic

www.ingramcontent.com/pod-product-compliance
Lightning Source LLC
Chambersburg PA
CBHW072006290426
44109CB00018B/2155